Date: 2/22/12

658 FOX
Fox, Jeffrey J.,
How to be a fierce
competitor : what winning

"What a fun and exciting and inspiring book. I read it in a single sitting. It's a must-read for any leader, in any organization, at any level, especially in these tough times."

—Jim Donald, former president and CEO of Starbucks

"It's easy to be a competitor when times are great and everyone is feeling good. What separates the winners from the losers, however, is what they do when times are tough. If you want to respond to tough times like a winner, this is the book for you!"

—Chris Widener, author, *The Art of Influence* and *The Angel Inside*

"Fox's principles on how to compete are clear, immediately usable, and will have high impact."

—Jack Stahl, former president and COO, The Coca-Cola Company and former CEO, Revlon

"*How to Be a Fierce Competitor* is great—focused, disciplined, practical. I learned a lot by reading it and it was a lot of fun!"

—Harry Kraemer, Jr., professor at Northwestern University's Kellogg School of Management and former chairman and CEO of Baxter International

Also by Jeffrey J. Fox

HOW TO BE A FIERCE COMPETITOR

WHAT WINNING COMPANIES AND GREAT MANAGERS DO IN TOUGH TIMES

Jeffrey J. Fox

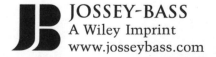

JOSSEY-BASS
A Wiley Imprint
www.josseybass.com

Published by Jossey-Bass
A Wiley Imprint
989 Market Street, San Francisco, CA 94103-1741—www.josseybass.com

Readers should be aware that Internet Web sites offered as citations and/or sources for
further information may have changed or disappeared between the time this was written
and when it is read.

Limit of Liability/Disclaimer of Warranty: While the publisher and author have used their
best efforts in preparing this book, they make no representations or warranties with respect
to the accuracy or completeness of the contents of this book and specifically disclaim any
implied warranties of merchantability or fitness for a particular purpose. No warranty may
be created or extended by sales representatives or written sales materials. The advice and
strategies contained herein may not be suitable for your situation. You should consult with
a professional where appropriate. Neither the publisher nor author shall be liable for any
loss of profit or any other commercial damages, including but not limited to special,
incidental, consequential, or other damages.

Jossey-Bass books and products are available through most bookstores. To contact
Jossey-Bass directly call our Customer Care Department within the U.S. at 800-956-7739,
outside the U.S. at 317-572-3986, or fax 317-572-4002.

Jossey-Bass also publishes its books in a variety of electronic formats. Some content that
appears in print may not be available in electronic books.

Library of Congress Cataloging-in-Publication Data
Fox, Jeffrey J., 1945–
  How to be a fierce competitor : what winning companies and great managers do in tough
times / Jeffrey J. Fox.—1st ed.
    p. cm.
  ISBN 978-0-470-40854-4 (cloth)
  1. Leadership. 2. Management. 3. Competition. 4. Business planning. 5. Business cycles.
I. Title.
  HD57.7.F694 2010
  658—dc22

                                                                    2009041372

Printed in the United States of America
FIRST EDITION
HB Printing 10 9 8 7 6 5 4 3 2 1

CONTENTS

CONTENTS

CONTENTS

To Luca Moe, Bella Ella, The Bean, Jozzie, PJ, Lily, Cosette, Madelaine, Chumley, Squid, Stella, Maple, Ridley, Buddha Blue, Zoe, and Sammy

Preface

There are hundreds of Fierce Competitor best practices in this book. Open to any page and put your finger on any sentence or two. If you are not using that best practice you touch, consider starting. If you are using that best practice, good, but flip the page.

Thank you for investing your time and money in this book. May your returns be infinite.

JJF

ACKNOWLEDGMENTS

Doris Michaels and Delia Berrigan Fakis, uber-agents in the DSM Literary Agency in New York City.

Karen Murphy, Senior Editor and whip-cracking author-wrangler, and everyone else on the terrific Jossey-Bass team, particularly Mark Karmendy.

Heather Belko Fox, tireless transcriber of countless pages, drafts, edits, and re-edits for most of the books in the Fox Business Library series.

HOW TO BE A FIERCE COMPETITOR

CHAPTER 1

THE FIERCE COMPETITOR COMPANY

Fierce competitor companies relentlessly, tirelessly, continuously do whatever they legally can to pursue and capture every profitable customer. They never stop innovating. They never stop selling, reaching out, and communicating to their markets. They train, train, train, and execute, execute, execute. They never stop ripping out waste and bad costs. Fierce competitor companies play to win. They compete for every inch of shelf space, every customer purchase, every first look and last look. They want every good customer, every sale, every penny in every pocketbook.

Fierce competitor companies have peerless customer service, amazing innovation, price leadership, highest-quality image, strong market share position, and great brand names; they are "most admired" by industry followers; and they make money.

Fierce competitors focus on their customers and their competitors. They watch everything their customers and competitors do. If a competitor is doing something that appeals to customers, the killer competitors will do something similar, but better. They often know more about their competitors than their competitors' own employees do.

The fierce competitor companies create jobs and add employees. Their marketplace success funds payrolls and benefit plans, creating prosperity for families and communities. Their purchasing budgets sustain thousands of suppliers and the suppliers' stakeholders. Their profits create value for share owners, pension plans, and retirement accounts. Their tax payments and philanthropy support school systems, police departments, Little Leagues, and hospitals.

These companies are ethical, honest, compliant with regulations, and model citizens.

They are sometimes feared and always watched by their competitors. They are loved by their customers. They are easy to do business with, but they never take it easy. If the rest of the industry starts work at 8:30 AM, they are in by 7:00 AM. If everyone else closes on Sundays, they are open. If the other guy wings it, the fierce competitors plan their moves with care.

It is tough to be a tough competitor. Fierce competitors often require more sacrifice than ordinary players. Fierce competitors know that happy, rested employees are most productive, and they work at morale building, but they never lower the performance bar. Never.

If you or your company is not a fierce competitor, then hope one never enters your industry, your space, your market.

As you will read, fierce competitors do unusual things—often spectacular, hard-to-believe, bold actions— to get customers, to get market share, to win.

Some of their stories may sound like urban legends, but they're not. They are what you need to be doing, how you need to be thinking, the risks you need to take, and if you want to gain market share, seize opportunity, and win when the stakes are at their highest, read on.

CHAPTER 2

Bad Times Are Good Times

Good, always-surviving, fierce competitors hunger for new sales, new customers, new revenues, new products, new talent, new technologies, new geographies, new channels to markets, new brands. They are always alert and ever on the lookout for assets of all kinds that they can use to strengthen their position in the marketplace.

The savvy, smart, well-led companies see bad times as a good time to gain market share, to out-fox the competition.

Fierce competitors ...

- aggressively pursue underserved customers.
- market to brand-indifferent customers and work mightily to make them brand-loyal.

- go after the other companies' dissatisfied, angry customers.
- buy under-priced hard assets.
- build capacity.
- hire newly available human talent.
- acquire product licenses, anxious good suppliers, undermarketed products, new wholesalers and distributors, and core-relevant acquisitions.

They go after market share and emerge from the downturn ahead of companies that pull back and play it safe.

CHAPTER 3

HUSTLE. HUSTLE. HUSTLE.

———

From the economic panic of 1823 through the Great Depression and the twelve recessions since 1955, the facts are indisputable: those companies that outsell, outmarket, out-train, out-innovate, and out-hustle their competition emerge from the downturn in a stronger market share and profit position than do those companies that hunker down.

Tough economic times are the perfect times to get new customers, launch new products, build inexpensive capacity. The marketplace is not as crowded with other sellers. Your ads are more prominent. Customers have more time to talk and to evaluate products—especially those that cut costs, boost revenues, and make the customer more competitive. Customers favor the company that visits them over the company that does not.

Two companies competed to sell specialized stencil machines used in the sign-making business. Due to "market conditions," the larger company cut its travel budget for sales people, significantly reducing the number of visits the sales force could make to current and new customers. On hearing that news, the CEO of the significantly smaller company sensed an opportunity and went into marketing overdrive. He met with his sales force and offered to increase commissions on selling products that were strategic to the bigger competitor. He offered one-time bonuses for every new customer the sales people switched to his company. He offered one-time bonuses for every deal closed on a Saturday. He added money to the travel budget as long as it was spent on breakfasts, lunches, or dinners, but only and always with customers.

The CEO hired one new person whose full-time job was to call customers and set up sales appointments for the sales people. The small company reached out to every possible customer, letting them know the company was increasing customer service levels and offering repairs on machines the big competitor sold, and now had a "no questions asked" warranty policy. The CEO notified all of his machine component suppliers of his plan. In exchange for the promise of increased parts volume, he negotiated paying in sixty days versus forty.

The CEO knew the larger competitor was an established company with good customer loyalty. He personally called the competitor's biggest customers to suggest that if their loyalty was greater to the sales person who called on them than it was to the larger company, he would consider hiring that sales person.

The CEO repeated and repeated his locker room speech: "We do not have 100-percent market share. There is business to get. Go get it."

The CEO later marveled at the situation. "If our competitor had done what we did, it might have put us out of business. It certainly would have hurt us. They had the money, the customers, everything. Now we do."

Don't hide from the customers. Don't hunker down in a hole. Don't go dark to the market.

Call one more customer.

Pay 1 percent more.

Add one more hour to your day.

Send one more email.

Take a chance.

In tough times the tough don't *start* selling; they *ratchet up* their selling. Fierce competitors put more people out in the field selling. They make it possible for sales people to make more money, not less. They invest scarce dollars to visit and meet more customers. They don't "save" money by quarantining their sales people, by cutting advertising, by reducing customer service reps.

Fierce competitors go for the business when the other companies are giving up on the business.

CHAPTER 4

LEADERSHIP IS NOT "PUSHERSHIP"

I t is said that in WWII Field Marshall Erwin Rommel, the Desert Fox, Germany's greatest general, knew whether the looming battle would be won or lost as he looked into his commander's eyes. "I knew the outcome because their eyes mirrored mine." Rommel lost very few battles, but his message is clear: a leader's attitude, posture, presence send signals that the organization correctly processes.

Great leaders will exhibit levels of confidence that exceed levels of certainty. They look into the mirror until they see victory peering back. They lead the organization with confidence, even when uncertain. They are sometimes fearful but always fearless. They may be overwhelmed, but never daunted, always willing.

The first leadership is self-leadership.

Leaders set winning examples that employees can emulate.

Field Marshall Rommel told his commanders: "Be an example to your men, in your duty and in private life. Let the troops see that you don't spare yourself in your endurance of fatigue and privation. Always be tactful and well-mannered and teach your subordinates to do the same. Avoid excessive sharpness or harshness of voice, which usually indicates a man who has shortcomings to hide." Leaders take note.

True leaders don't push the soldiers, the employees, the sales people. Leaders push themselves. They push themselves through the tough times into the good times.

Leadership is "Pullership."

CHAPTER 5

THE DIFFERENCE BETWEEN LEADERS AND MANAGERS

J ob titles, media profiles, membership in King Arthur's Court—these give not a clue as to what makes a leader or manager.

Leaders can be good or bad. Managers can be effective or not. Leaders can bring victory or march, head high, into the valley of death. Leaders can be accidental, appointed, elected, promoted, proven or not.

Great leaders supported by superb managers is what the executive team shareholders want. Leaders, regardless of title or job function, can be found at every level of the organization. Same with managers.

The single biggest difference between leaders and managers is the tolerance for ambiguity. Leaders can deal with ambiguity, can deal with not having all the facts, not having all the data. Leaders make decisions, big decisions, midcrisis decisions, without certainty of the outcome. Managers don't.

Ironically, it is in crisis, when thinking and reflection are most needed, that fast decisions are required. It is in crisis that the most needed facts and information are not available. Managers are immobilized by the blank page, the shattered compass, the blackout.

Leaders respond and act. They may be wrong, but they don't dither, dawdle, delay. They decide. Managers may have the best MBA education possible, but they measure metrics, analyze, maintain the status quo, and, as they love to say, "do deep data dives." Data dives are good, necessary, professional, but when you come up for air, that's it. Decide.

Smart, realistic, objective homework and analysis of all available facts, data, research is a fundamental of good business stewardship. But during a crisis, tough times, when the need for guiding information is penultimate, but it's not at the ready, and when there is no time to dwell, you want a leader pulling the trigger, not some guy calling headquarters for signed-off detailed instructions.

Note how often in a tied-game soccer shootout, shooter number five, the game winner or loser, may not be the team captain, may not be the leading scorer, but he or she is a leader.

No ambiguity. Make the shot or lose the game.

CHAPTER 6

KNOW YOUR COMPANY'S RAISON D'ETRE

T hat marvelous French term *raison d'être* means "reason to be." Everyone in the company must know why the company exists—its raison d'être. Everyone must know what business they are in. All companies exist to get and keep profitable customers. The getting and keeping of profitable customers requires giving customers what they want and need at prices that exceed all company costs. Customers want to feel good or they need to solve a problem or some combination of the two. These are the only reasons any customer buys anything.

Winning companies understand this buying phenomenon. Thus they don't sell products and services; they sell outcomes. Great marketers sell what the customer gets from the product.

Rolex doesn't sell time, it sells status. Timex doesn't sell status, it sells time. Titleist doesn't sell golf balls, it sells lower golf scores. Harley-Davidson doesn't sell motorcycles, it sells individualism. Pfizer doesn't sell pills, it sell cures.

If Pfizer were in the business of selling pills, it wouldn't make vaccines or serums, and it wouldn't acquire companies that solve other medical problems. Every Pfizer scientist—and every Pfizer sales person—knows what business he or she is in, why the company exists.

Knowing why your company exists keeps your company in existence.

CHAPTER 7

MANAGE AS YOU WOULD INVEST

G ood companies are thoughtful and discriminating as to how they allocate time, people, money.

If, as an investor, you had the choice to invest your personal money in the stock of a growing, high-potential company or in a stodgy, low-performing company, where would you put your money? This question is supposed to be rhetorical, but it isn't.

Most of the time, if not all the time, you would invest your money in the company that is the high performer. Yet every single day CEOs, and the managers CEOs oversee, knowingly violate the "invest in performance" rule. CEOs allow managers to spend more time with low-performing, problem employees than they do with their best people. Every day sales managers invest their time with the bottom sales people and practically ignore their superstars. Every day managers cut the marketing, selling, and training budgets in their strong businesses and in their growing product lines to "offset" underperforming parts of the company.

Just as the smart investor would never knowingly invest in a doggy business, so too should great leaders not invest the company's capital or the company's management time in low-performing people or units. Instead, you should pour the coals into the growth opportunities. You should overinvest in business and products and brands and people that have big potential.

Some managers starve good businesses to hit short-term profit goals, such as the misleading "quarterly number." Choking a good business, even temporarily, to hit a Wall Street mandate is a mistake. Cutting the funding for activities that fuel sales growth and fuel innovation slows growth, dulls innovation, retards market share penetration, and provides catch-up time for competitors.

Hitting or not hitting Wall Street's calendars has zero effect on the long-term value of the stock. If you sell hard every day and make money every day, your company will do fine. Robbing the rich opportunity to cover poor performers is a losing strategy. The rich will get poorer, and the poor performers will not get better.

Good companies and great leaders invest to strengthen their enterprise and to take advantage of competitors that do not.

A big regional bank suddenly found itself in big trouble. The local economy was in recession. Commercial loans and mortgages were going into default at a dismaying rate. The panicked bank management ordered cuts in advertising, hiring, and selling expenses across all departments and business units. Despite the economy, the trust department was generating substantial revenues and profits. The success was tied directly to a unique direct mail program aimed at wealthy individuals. The head of the trust department argued in vain that cutting the direct mail program would hurt business and worsen the bank's problem. She argued that the trust department's profits could save the bank. Deaf ears. Dumb ears. Bank leaders should have doubled, tripled, quadrupled the direct mail program budget. The program was cut. New trust revenues plummeted. The bank could not recover.

Invest your company's money where it gets the highest return. Don't cut investments in projects that are generating a good return on the investment. Don't invest in losing situations. Don't let losing situations drain investment from winning situations. Invest your time with people who are winners. Invest your time with your highest-performing sales people, with your most creative marketing people, and with your most inventive innovators.

Then watch your investment pay.

17

CHAPTER 8

"I Visit Customers in Stores"

I t was 1933—the middle of the Great Depression. Yet immediately after the repeal of Prohibition, Ernest and Julio Gallo started the E. & J. Gallo Winery with $900 of their own money and a $5,000 loan. Ernest was twenty-four. Julio was twenty-three. At the time, there were eight hundred competing wineries in California alone. Thirty years later, the two brothers, sons of Italian immigrants, had built E. & J. Gallo into the largest wine maker and wine seller in the world. Ernest was the marketing savant behind the creation of this awesome enterprise.

What did this great leader do in bad times, good times, all times to win in a crushingly competitive marketplace?

In the early 1960s, Legh Knowles, then a sales manager for E. & J. Gallo, received notice that Ernest would be visiting Cincinnati, Ohio, on the Thursday before Labor Day weekend. Legh was to show Ernest the market. Ernest outlined his weekend plan.

Legh said, "But Ernest, this is Labor Day weekend."

"Exactly," Ernest answered.

And they proceeded to call on over a hundred stores and wholesaler branches.

Ernest peppered store managers, clerks, and customers with questions. "What products are selling?" "Why do you think that product is selling?" "What do we need to do to help you sell more, to make you more money?" "What do you think of the brand name...of the label...of the price...of the taste?" "Can I count on you to push Gallo wines?"

Ernest Gallo knew that the secrets to business success are discovered in the marketplace, not in the office. Ernest also knew that the word would spread that the boss worked on Labor Day. When the boss labors on Labor Day, everyone else works harder on Monday and Wednesday and Friday.

Thirty years later, when Michael Mondavi, son of the charismatic Napa Valley wine pioneer Robert Mondavi, met Ernest Gallo, Ernest asked Michael, "Do you know what I do?"

Michael answered, "Yes, you run the largest winery in the country."

"No," Ernest said. "I go out and visit customers in stores."

CHAPTER 9

ALWAYS ANSWER
THE PHONE

Charley Boyle was the general manager of the Advanced Polymers Division of the Furon Corporation, located in Hoosick Falls, New York. The factory was in an isolated area of northern New York. It was 6:10 PM on July 2 when the phone rang. Charley was the last person in the office. Everyone else was getting ready for the Fourth of July holiday. The phone kept ringing until Charley answered. The person calling spoke haltingly, in heavily-accented English. It was difficult to understand even half of what the caller was saying, but Charley patiently pieced together the story.

The caller's boss had tasked him with finding a company that could make fire-resistant tent fabric. The caller had been contacting companies all over the world.

The company's West Coast headquarters, after hanging up on the caller a few times, had finally provided the number of Charley's factory. After an exasperating ten minutes, Charley told the caller, "Yes. We can make fire-proof tent material." Although it was nearly 1:30 AM in the caller's country, he pleaded with Charley to hold on until he could find his boss.

That the caller's boss was still looking to find a supplier at 1:30 AM was a buy signal to Charley. *These guys must have a big problem*, Charley thought.

The caller's boss got on the phone and in respectable English politely introduced himself and his employer.

"I work for his Majesty, the King of Saudi Arabia. Thank you for taking our call. I must tell you that we know yours is not the only company that makes tent cloth, but you are the only person we have found that would listen to our plight. As a matter of fact, every other company hung up in the first few minutes."

King of Saudi Arabia ... our plight, Charley thought.

"How may I help you?" Charley asked.

The caller explained that the annual pilgrimage to Mecca would take place in December and that it was the King's personal responsibility to ensure the safety and welfare of those visiting Mecca. The kingdom supplied tents, in all sizes and complexities, to the pilgrims.

"Why do you want fire-proof tent materials?" Charley asked.

"Last year there was a tent fire and a number of pilgrims perished. The King has instructed me to eliminate the tent-fire hazard."

"How much material will you need?"

"I'm not certain, but we will provide thousands of tents. At least five hundred thousand square meters, I would estimate."

Charley clenched the phone. Five hundred thousand square meters was a huge deal, and three times the capacity of his facility.

"Do you have a budget in mind to pay for the material?" Charley asked.

"The King does not put a price on the lives of people conducting their holy pilgrimage."

"When would you like to meet?" Charley asked.

"Can you meet our needs?" the caller inquired.

"We'll find a way," Charley responded.

"When can you visit?"

"I will fly to Riyadh tomorrow."

They discussed the travel logistics, hotel, meeting times. That night Charley packed for a visit to a place he'd never been. He flew to Saudi Arabia the next day. And while all his competitors, who had hung up on the King's caller or who were too important to answer the phone, were having hot dogs and ice cream on Independence Day, Charley closed a multiyear, multimillion-dollar deal. His next big sale was to convince the Furon Corporation's board of directors to trust the word of the

King and immediately invest in capacity to fulfill the order.

When asked how he accomplished the single biggest sale in the history of his company, Charley said simply, "I just answered the phone."

It starts with picking up the phone but also includes doing careful needs analysis, qualifying the customer, following up with deep due diligence as to the legitimacy of the customer, and leaping into action:

- Never let anyone outwork you. It is noteworthy that he or she who is in the proverbial "right place at the right time" is the hardest worker.
- Everyone is a possible customer. Don't be biased against a possible customer by the way they talk, what they wear, or where they live.
- Make the sale, get the business. Figure out how to deliver later. Getting the sale is the hard part.
- And always answer the phone.

CHAPTER 10

PILE UP CASH

C ash is always king, but in tough times cash is the king and his court. Cash can be a company's lifeblood, meeting payroll, buying supplies, keeping the business alive. Cash can also be a killer competitive weapon. It can be used to buy assets and supplier products at deep discounts. It can be used to make acquisitions at distressed prices. Cash can be used to outspend and out-market competitors and gain critical share. Cash can be used to offer liberal payment terms to win over that big important new customer.

Winning companies are managed to maximize cash. They look at all possible sources of cash, and they craft plans to increase cash. The primary sources of cash are:

- *Operations.* Good companies work to increase prices, increase unit sales, and cut costs. Revenues minus all expenses is cash.

24

- *Lenders.* Banks and financiers are in business to make loans. Smart companies often borrow money at interest rates that are lower than the company's internal rate of return on cash invested in the business.
- *Lessors.* Leasing equipment uses less cash than buying equipment.
- *Credit cards.* Even Fortune 100 companies purchase with credit cards. Do so *if* you can pay it off at the end of the month or if your interest rate is low.
- *Stockholders.* Companies sell stock to the public to raise cash.
- *Issuing bonds.* Bonds are commonly used to fund long-term projects, to retire higher-interest-rate loans.
- *Collecting accounts receivables.* The faster a company collects what is owed, the faster they'll have the cash. Winning companies employ well-trained, nice, cheerful, courteous, polite, persistent, and empathetic people to speed payment.
- *Stretching accounts payable.* The longer you take to pay, the longer you hold onto cash. Accounts payable management requires keen sensitivity: crucial suppliers, that is, "good" suppliers, should be paid as soon as possible. Suppliers that can live with delayed payments may have to wait.

- *C.O.D.* Cash paid on delivery is cash in hand.
- *Eliminating theft.* Businesses that have a high percentage of cash transactions have to watch the till with care. Cash has a tendency to stick to greedy fingers.
- *Selling assets.* Selling a building for $5,000,000, for example, and leasing it back from the owner for $50,000 a year generates cash.
- *Getting return on investments.* The interest on unbreakable long-term instruments can be used in the business.
- *Rents.* Renting or subletting unused, unsellable real estate, such as extra offices or half-full warehouses, is a source of cash.
- *Cutting dividends.* In tough times the shareholders may have to forgo dividends to help the company survive.

A company can continue without profits, but it cannot live without cash.

All times are the times to pile up cash and build reserves.

CHAPTER 11

BE EVER FEARFUL

The father of modern venture capital, Georges Doriot, uttered the famous quote, "Someone, somewhere, is making a product that will make your product obsolete." The message: never stop improving, adapting, innovating. Be ever fearful of the obsolescing technology, the vanishing market, the changing playing fields.

Being ever fearful makes you ever watchful. Watch what your customers are doing. Watch what your competitors are doing. Watch what the regulators and governments are plotting. Watch how best practice organizations are improving. Visit your sales offices, distributors, stores. Talk to everyone in the company. Watch and listen.

Look and listen with clear-headed realism. Don't flinch from the facts. Don't ignore unsettling evidence of trouble or problems. The dirtier the details, the more ominous the potential threat, the more important it is for leaders to get involved. Get involved early and intensely.

In 1986, David Halberstam wrote a wonderful book, *The Reckoning. The Reckoning* outlined what American car makers were doing wrong and what non-American car makers were doing right. *The Reckoning* was predictive and should have been the catalyst for instant strategy and cultural changes in Detroit. Typically, instead of dealing forthright with a fearful future, American automobile executives went ostrichical, burying their heads in the sands of yesterday.

Be ever alert, on guard, at the watchtower. Never get complacent. Always be focused, thinking, and solution finding. Constantly generate ideas and new strategies. Ever wary is ever successful.

CHAPTER 12

Show Fearlessness

From 1945 to 1989 Poland was under communist control. In 1979, Pope John Paul II undertook a historic nine-day pilgrimage through Poland, including delivering a breathtaking sermon at Victory Square in Warsaw. That visit sparked a peaceful uprising that eventually ended communism in Poland and in most of Eastern Europe. That the revolution was peaceful is extraordinary, as the Soviet Union always marched to squash any anticommunist, pro-freedom movements. In the early 1980s the Polish Solidarity movement angered Moscow. There were Soviet threats of an invasion.

Perhaps legend, but never denied, was a report that Pope John Paul II—who was born Karol Wojtyla in Wadowice, Poland—quietly sent a private note to Leonid Brezhnev, leader of the Soviet Union. Pope John Paul warned Brezhnev that if the Soviet Union invaded Poland then he, the Pope, would be in the front line, shoulder-to-shoulder with his fellow Poles. The Soviets quieted their rhetoric.

Word of the note flashed through Poland. The Poles knew they could have no stronger ally. John Paul's personal fearlessness ignited a national fearlessness that communism could not quell.

Years later, another Soviet leader, Mikhail Gorbachev, said, "The collapse of the Iron Curtain would have been impossible without John Paul II."

Leaders face the fearsome. They face the facts. They are tough-minded realists. Leaders let the employees know the situation, the dimensions of the challenge. True leaders do not parse words and spin, as do politicians. They tell the truth as they know it. They stay calm. They are resolute.

Leaders tell the company what to do to surmount the challenge. They ask for help, for support, for cooperation, sometimes for sacrifice. And if there is to be sacrifice, such as pay cuts, the leader's compensation is the first one cut.

Fearlessness is infectious. If the leader stands in the front lines, facing slow economies, angry customers, merciless competitors, then so too will the rest of the company.

CHAPTER 13

PLAY "WHAT IF?" GAMES

—

Knowing that the competition may be plotting some kind of an offensive or attack, the fierce competitors play "what if?" games. Executives and key employees are grouped into teams. Each team is named a competitor. Each team, as a competitor, does an analysis of its strengths and their own company's weaknesses, opportunities, environment changes, everything. Each team is tasked with developing strategies that may catch their own company off guard, or would weaken their own company.

After the business plans are presented, the team members are rearranged into new teams. The new teams, now back in their own company, develop counterattack strategies. Some counterattack strategies are immediately deployed. Others are in place to use in case the competitor makes a move.

The fierce competitors are constantly asking and answering "what if?" questions. What if our technology were instantly obsolesced? What if a new government regulation cripples our product? What if our smartest employees left to form a new company or went to a quasi-competitor? What if the market for our products booms, or flattens, or declines?

"What if?" games expose weaknesses, in both the company and the competitors. "What if?" games generate new thinking. They put managers into the minds of their competitors. They force management to consider all scenarios and to build response action plans. "What if?" games simulate the real thing.

Fierce competitors play "what if?" games, and they play to win.

CHAPTER 14

LEADERSHIP IS FULL DISCLOSURE

———

Especially in tough times, everyone who works at a company wants to know what is really happening. It is unnerving and time wasting to hear negative or positive news on the rumor mill. Leaders don't have to allay fears—fear can often provide focus. But leaders do have to allay false fears. They have to be in front of the gossips, the rumor mongers. People shouldn't hear it through the grapevine; they should hear the news, the information, from the leader. Leaders have to tell the truth, give facts. (Sometimes there are secrets that must be kept confidential, but this is rarer than is practiced.) Leaders have to get the employees to focus on the job, and an effective way to do that is to have an informed, intelligent, confident workforce.

Wired-in leaders know that there is always a rumor mill, always scuttlebutt. They know that it is rare that every employee gets perfect understanding of the unfolding events, the crisis, the issue. Leaders must create a "no-fire zone" atmosphere in which every employee can ask any question, question any decision, without career consequences. Great leaders know that they are not infallible, thus they crave the clarifying questions and opinions of everyone.

When employees, unions, partners, customers, suppliers learn that the leader is fair, honest, and forthcoming, problems are avoided, compromises possible.

- Be aware of the rumor mill—and head it off whenever possible.
- Create an open-door culture in which employees can come to you with questions without fear of reprisal.

Disclosure leads to deals.

CHAPTER 15

GET A KITCHEN CABINET

Good companies have great leadership, great CEOs. Leadership is a lonely job. Leaders are surrounded by ambitious executives who have private and personal agendas. They are surrounded by people who, even if they get along with each other, are rivals. These people are rivals for the leader's ear, for favor, for approval for all kinds of decisions—from asset and investment allocation to bonuses, promotions, new hires, and organizational changes.

If your company is public, or is a substantial not-for-profit organization, the leader reports to a board of directors. If the leader does not own the company, he or she is reporting to a board, to trustees, to some fiduciary. Good boards expect performance, and they see themselves more as watchdogs than as mentors. The stockholders are always impatient. The stockholders' mantra is *move the stock price, move the merchandise, make money, or move on!* And those fickle customers! If the leader is not also the company's product—as is a lawyer, for example—the customers don't care a whit about the guy.

The leader is surrounded, yet lonely. Leaders need people they can trust. They need people who can and will deliver the unvarnished truth, the organization scuttlebutt, reactions to ideas, solution suggestions. These people may be inside the organization or on the board, but most often they will be outsiders. These people are the leader's "kitchen cabinet."

The phrase "kitchen cabinet" dates from 1832, when President Andrew Jackson had three trusted friends who met with him frequently to advise on important and private issues. This group had more influence than did Jackson's official cabinet. To avoid detection the three advisors would come and go through the back door, in the kitchen.

Great leaders have a kitchen cabinet all through their career. The kitchen cabinet is often one person. One trusted confidant. One consigliere. One of wise counsel and advice. Get a good kitchen cabinet, and it won't matter how hot it gets in the kitchen.

CHAPTER 16

ALWAYS HAVE
A PLAN

R unning a business is like hosting a huge party—
such as a festival, wedding, or state dinner—at
which you want every invited guest to have a wonderful
time, to say good things, and to return if invited. The customers are the party guests. The products are the food,
entertainment, decorations, and friendly ambience. The
sales people are the hosts. There may even be a professional party planner. Without a good plan, without super
execution, the host's party will fail, and reputations will
be damaged.

Creating the business and marketing plan for the
company and the key products is like creating the plan
for the party. Planners list all the elements critical to
success, build in contingencies, try to think of everything,
calendarize and time events.

The business plan includes:

- Target customers (as in "desired guests," to continue the metaphor)
- Budget
- Dates
- Marketplace (as in the wedding venue)
- Lead time
- Market research (as in discovering that certain guests have food restrictions)
- Product (as in food, beverage, flowers)
- Communications (like invitations)
- Key people. In a wedding the waiters are sales people, the chefs are manufacturing, the parents are finance.
- Security

And so on.

If a success factor is in the plan, such as market research, then attention to every detail of the market research is crucial.

Fierce competitors always plan, and always execute, execute, execute the plan.

STAY OFF MAGAZINE COVERS

G reat leaders do not waste management and marketing time seeking to get on the cover of *Bossadacious* magazine. Instead, great leaders and managers care far more about getting stories of their products, grateful customers, and compelling case histories into the magazines and on television.

With the rare exception of building brand awareness, there is little good, and lots of bad, that comes from glowing executive profiles. Profiles are not a substitute for internal communications or for external advertising. Profiles give competitors clues as to strategy, spending, capital budgets, and upcoming products, and insight into key executive personalities and on succession and organizational issues. Profiles have to appear to be balanced, so the writer, interviewer, or commentator often throws in a caveat or a negative. This information is fodder for the analysts on the teams fighting to get your customers, your meal tickets, and your lunch.

- Don't give external speeches unless you are saying something to impress your customers.
- Don't politic for somebody running for office.
- Don't go to Davos or Aspen or wherever. Go to work.
- Don't go on boards unless there is an acceptable way to get other members as customers.
- Unless you plan to buy "five covers for your mother" (music aficionados will understand this reference), don't get your smiling face on the cover of any magazine.
- Don't give others an unearned edge. Rather, look for an edge, and use it. Celebrities love media coverage. CEOs love market coverage.

CHAPTER 18

"I NEVER MADE A DIME TALKING"

Sebastian Spering Kresge was one of America's many great leaders and business creators. He built the S. S. Kresge Corporation into the world's largest chain of "five-and-ten-cent" or "nickel-and-dime" stores. In 1962 he founded Kmart, which grew into a chain of over 1,400 stores.

The "K" in Kmart is for Kresge. In a significant co-incidence, another somewhat eponymously named corporation, Wal-Mart, was founded by Sam Walton also in 1962. And in 1962 Target stores began selling. By the 1990s these great merchandisers became the top three retailers in the United States.

Kresge started his dime stores purposefully to make products available and affordable to people of minimal and modest means. By helping those in need, Kresge amassed an immense fortune that funded his worldwide philanthropy.

S. S. Kresge was born and raised on a hardscrabble farm. When his stores reached $10 million in sales, he characterized the milestone as "100 million dimes." He was rigidly frugal, claiming he never spent more than "300 pennies for lunch" in his life. Yet he started his company by risking his entire savings of $8,000 (which he had made as a traveling salesman) to buy one store.

He had an early-to-bed, early-to-rise work ethic. His business creed was based on integrity, honesty, providing fair value, and respect for all, particularly employees (Kresge pioneered paid sick days and paid vacations).

One recipient of Mr. Kresge's generosity is Harvard Business School. In 1953 S. S. Kresge was invited to make a speech at the ribbon-cutting ceremony opening Kresge Hall. He stood. He looked upon the assemblage of future business leaders, all eagerly awaiting the words of wealth. Kresge said, "I never made a dime talking," and sat down.

Kresge's message was that action trumps words.

WACADAD: "Words are cheap and deeds are dear."

Act, do things, invent things, make things, sell things.

CHAPTER 19

NEVER TAKE YOUR HAND OFF THE TILLER

T he tiller is what the captain uses to steer the boat. The tiller can be a wooden bar in the stern of the boat. It can be a steering wheel in the cockpit. Whatever the technology, the tiller directs the boat.

Great captains never take their hand off the tiller in storms, crises, delicate situations.

Sailors, passengers sleep soundly as the boat plies the waters—as long as there is a hand on the tiller. The boat could be heading toward a mountainous rock and no one would stir—as long as there is a hand on the tiller. Even in the calmest of seas, if the captain, or whoever is driving the boat, lets go of the tiller, for even a second, and the boat shifts a bit, the sleepers snap awake. Something may be amiss.

The same phenomenon is true in companies. Employees know when the captain, the leader, takes his or her hand off the tiller. They sense that the company, like a sailboat, is adrift, off course, in trouble. People in the company will face any storm. Employees are not stupid. They just want to know what they should do. They want to be led. They want certainty of purpose in the people in charge.

Companies can deal with the sudden death or firing or exit of someone in leadership. Someone else takes the wheel, the tiller. Someone is in charge. Company people get rattled when the guy in charge abandons or abdicates his post. People worry that the ship will go aground, that the absent captain knows a terrible secret, that an unknown danger lurks.

In tough times, effective leaders …

- take action.
- stay visible.
- are openly approachable.
- set performance examples.
- communicate constantly.
- stay calm.
- blame nothing and no one.
- ask for support.

The burden of leadership is to safely steer the company past Scylla and Charybdis, and through the wild waters of Cape Horn. You can't steer if you don't have the wheel.

CHAPTER 20

CONTROL OR ROLL

C ontrol what you can control. Managers can control most internal decisions and activities. You can control budgets, who to hire, when to launch a new product, brand-name choices, advertising messages, and where to locate manufacturing facilities, distribution centers, and sales offices. You can control how much internal control is optimal and how to loosen controls that fetter employee creativity.

You can't control the competition, the government, changes in demographics, the economy. You can plan for changes in the business environment, but you can't control that environment. You can predict changes. You must plan for changes. But you can't control the changes.

Inability to control is not a reason for paralysis or inaction. Your competition has no more control than do you. Stay cool. Develop contingency plans. Be alert.

Be ready to deploy. Roll with that which is beyond your control.

When it is raining, the Chinese have a roll-with-it expression: "Let it rain." You can't control the rain. So roll with it. Let it rain. But you can control whether or not the company has umbrellas, raincoats, storm water catchment basins, levees.

If you can't control an event, have a plan to contain the fallout.

CHAPTER 21

GET OUT
OF THE OFFICE

W hen times are tough, great leaders spend even more time in the marketplace than they do in good times. Leaders set the example and get out of the comfortable confines of their spare and spartan offices and go into the battlefield of rejection, complaints, and competitors. Great leaders are often the fiercest of competitors. They fearlessly call on angry customers, on prospects, look for ways to do business, and ask for the order. They call on customers, especially important customers who may be at risk. In particular, they call on upset and dissatisfied customers. They call on suppliers to find ways to improve quality, to reduce costs, to improve business for everyone. They call on distributors, wholesalers, retailers, and all resellers, and exhort them to sell more product, to stock more product, to merchandise key products, to put up displays, to run co-op advertising, to book more joint sales calls, to train more sales people.

They call on the owners and managers of potential acquisitions or joint ventures.

Leaders visit their sales people, make sales calls with them. They go where the business is, not where the resorts are. They walk their office halls and factory floors. They visit every nook and cranny of their organization. Leaders spend time communicating to employees, in person, by video, by email, in town hall meetings.

Spending time in the office insulates leaders and managers. Absent marketplace reality, without customer facts, the conversation gets inbred. Groupthink takes over. The smarter the group, the more brilliant the think. Rationales for decision making are by hunch instead of by homework and research. You can't hear what customers are muttering and mumbling with the office door closed. You can't see a customer take your product off the shelf, study the label, and put the package back. You can't observe a sales person meeting a customer completely unprepared, unprofessional, and untrained, unless you are with the guy. You can't see why the retailer convinces the customer to buy the competitor's product unless you are in the store.

- The more senior the executive, the more important it is to regularly meet with customers and sales people.
- Sales call reports should be four or five sentences: result of call, next step, help needed. Management must read these.
- Management must read and react to all letters, emails, and complaints from customers.
- Management must read and react to all internet reviews and blogs.
- Management must visit competitors' stores, outlets, websites.

Firsthand marketplace knowledge is a competitive advantage.

CHAPTER 22

WALK AROUND
THE COMPANY

In his classic business book *In Search of Excellence*, Tom Peters coined the directional acronym "MBWA"—management by walking around. Tom is still right.

Walking around the company makes the leader visible, approachable. Walking around keeps people from fooling around. Everyone is at their best when the top people are actively engaged in the work process, in observing, being available to help. Walking around enables the perceptive leader to judge the organization's psyche, morale, readiness, toughness, inventiveness. He or she may hear valuable scuttlebutt, rumors, misinformation. Always being around is a way for managers to sense the cultural pulse of the company. Being in the fray is another way to spot future stars, notice behavior issues, observe interpersonal chemistry challenges.

Walking around does not mean you have to help load the trucks or solve the big marketing problem, but it does mean you will know who are the good truck loaders and good marketing mavens, and who are not.

Leaders walk, visit, watch, ask, listen, hear, help, praise, give credit, say "Thanks."

Walk around the company. It is good exercise.

CHAPTER 23

NEVER FORGET THE THIRD SHIFT

A t a high-growth manufacturing company, sales were so robust that the company was at full capacity. Its production line was working twenty-four hours a day. The first shift works from 7:00 AM to 3:00 PM, the second shift from 3:30 PM to 11:30 PM, and the third shift, the night shift, from midnight to 6:45 AM. The people on the third shift work when the sun doesn't shine, when most of the world is asleep.

The CEO, newly promoted to his position, gathered his nine direct reports and announced a celebration.

"We are going to celebrate my promotion at a luncheon tomorrow night."

"Don't you mean tomorrow afternoon?" someone asked.

"Nope. A big barbecue celebration lunch tomorrow night."

"But tomorrow is Friday. Who serves lunch at night?" another asked.

"I do."

"You do?"

"Correct. Tomorrow at 3:00 AM the third shift breaks for lunch. And I am throwing a TGIF barbeque celebration. And I'm cooking. And you are all invited."

The following night, at three in the morning, the new CEO served grilled chicken and hamburgers to every person working the third shift. The CEO was dumbfounded that none of his direct reports had taken him up on his invitation. He introduced himself and shook hands with everyone. He asked about their jobs, their families. He thanked the people for their hard work, for their attention to quality, for their safety record, and for their sterling attendance record. He gave every person his private phone number with an open invitation to call him with any problems or ideas.

The following Monday afternoon the CEO arranged a five-minute meeting with his nine direct reports.

"None of you showed up for my promotion party," he started. "You missed all the fun. You missed meeting the people who get the shipments out on time each month that help you earn part of your bonus. You missed meeting the lady whose idea to reorganize the filling machines saves us $50,000 a year. You missed her smile when I gave her an on-the-spot bonus and gave her the parking space by the door for a month. And you missed meeting someone who may be the next plant manager, maybe VP of manufacturing someday."

"Now my feeling is that the third shift is just as important as any other part of this company, and that every individual that works on the third shift is as important as anyone else. Got it?"

The "third shift" is a metaphor for those people and groups of people who toil in relative anonymity in the organization. They may be the workers on the night shift; the scientists in distant labs, behind locked doors, working on the next breakthroughs; the customer service people dealing with problems and one irate customer after another; the field repair people fixing critical customer machinery on a weekend or holiday; the caregivers that empty bed pans. These people may not be omnipresent, but they are critical to the continuing success of the company. Great managers recognize such people, give them credit, give sincere thank-yous.

Every contributor counts. Count on every contributor, every employee.

CHAPTER 24

BE OBSESSIVE ABOUT
EXECUTION

B e obsessive when it comes to daily execution of
your company's winning strategies. Danaher Corp
is obsessive about executing its Danaher Business System, a never-ending, methodological, no-detail-too-small
strategy for reducing product manufacturing costs and
eliminating scrap, redundant labor, nonproductive time,
and waste of every kind. Ergo, one of the most successful and best managed corporations in the world.

UPS is obsessed with its evergreen goal of delivering
more packages per driver, per route, per vehicle — on time
and undamaged. Literally every move and every step a
driver makes is studied to improve efficiency. Trucks are
electronically routed to always turn right to save time

and fuel. Trucks are loaded to match the routing: last on, first off. UPS is a technical giant innovator in storage, distribution, logistics. UPS asks, "What can Brown do for you?" and they are not kidding.

There is a global big-name company that serves millions of consumers every day of the week. The products are primarily food and drink. As it is for many companies in this type of business, cleanliness is an obsession. Clean hands, clean countertops, clean tables, clean uniforms, clean everything—and clean, clean bathrooms.

The global company's CEO was rarely in his office. He was omnipresent in the marketplace, visiting outlets, talking to customers and associates, meeting with suppliers. As he drove up to a brand-new outlet, two days into its "Grand Opening" week, he saw lines of customers waiting to be served. The workers were working, really working. The CEO arrived unannounced. During his apparently casual walk-through he stopped to scrub clean a soiled countertop. Next, he looked at the mandatory bathroom hourly cleaning schedule. The staff was some time behind; signatures indicated the bathrooms were being checked, but not hourly. Too busy serving customers. He then inspected the bathrooms. One stall had been grossly soiled. The CEO recoiled, hoping no customers had entered before him. The CEO knew the standardized layout of the stores and immediately went to the janitorial closet and got the mops, the soaps, the gloves. Thirty minutes later the bathroom had been obsessively sanitized.

Two days later, the competent and able store manager received a handwritten note from the CEO:

> Congratulations on how wonderfully you and your staff handled the overwhelming crowd of customers on June 17. I was especially impressed with Dorothy on the cash register. Great smile. Great manner. In a busy place, a lot can happen in just an hour. That's why we need you to be sure the bathrooms are inspected at least hourly. We avoided a potential public relations disaster at 11:18 AM on June 17. God forbid that a customer, a health inspector, or a foods editor from the newspaper might have gotten there before me. Keep up your outstanding customer service. I appreciate it.
>
> Cleaningly yours,
>
> CEO
>
> P.S. Check the supplies closet. You may need to replace the gloves. JD

Even though this CEO sends thousands of notes to appreciative associates, most of them handwritten, this one is a Hall-of-Famer.

- If something, such as cleanliness, is a success factor, then every detail about keeping the place clean is important.
- If the CEO can clean a toilet, then everyone else can clean a toilet.
- Leaders establish a performance culture by doing what they expect others to do.

The fierce competitors are obsessed, possessed, with execution of their game plan for success.

CHAPTER 25

GET RID OF
EXECUTIVE PARKING
SPACES

W hy should certain top executives have reserved parking spaces? Is it because they are chronically late to work and all the good spots will be taken? Or is it because they are better, more important, than disposable workers?

What is more important: a two-dollar spark plug, or a thousand-dollar steering system? If either part is inoperable you can't drive the car. In good companies all parts of the machine work together and are dependent on each other.

Ethan was a new hire. It was his first day on the job. He was considered a crackerjack, a fast-tracker. He was on a leadership program that included programmed stints in marketing, sales, finance, and manufacturing.

The head of human resources was giving this new guy the grand tour of the office compound. The tour included a glass walkway that connected two buildings and crossed over a parking lot below.

"See those parking spaces down there?" the human resources VP asked. "You do well here, and someday your initials will be on one of those spaces."

"Are those spaces for the top people?" Ethan asked.

"Yep. CEO, COO, head of sales, so on."

"Why does the company give special parking places to the top people?"

"It is considered to be a valuable perk, something special that goes with the title."

"Valuable? How much are the spots worth?" Ethan inquired.

The VP laughed. "That's a good question."

"I'll sell you my future space for a thousand dollars."

The VP laughed again.

Fourteen years later Ethan turned down the reserved parking space that accompanied his C-Suite promotion. "Give it to someone who needs to park closer to the office," he said.

Four years after that, Ethan was the new president of the company. The prime parking spaces were still reserved, but now they were reserved for customers.

The new president's rationale was clear:

- If visiting customers first see a row of expensive cars, they may assume the company's prices are too high.
- If suppliers first see a line of flashy cars, they will assume the company can afford to receive higher prices.
- If customers think that some people in the company are more important than others, they will only want to talk to the "important, high-ranking" people, and look to bypass sales and customer service to get concessions from top management.
- A good customer experience starts with the hospitality of a convenient parking space.
- Special parking spaces signal special people. The "special people" are customers.
- Employee morale may suffer if some people are rewarded because of job title, and not because of performance.
- Even if it costs $1.00 a year to repaint parking space initials or to change the signs, it is a waste of time and money.
- An egalitarian company culture, where everybody is treated equally, encourages objective feedback, creative thinking, and open door communication.
- A company's VIP's are its customers. Customers get the VIP parking spaces.

FIGHT
UNIONIZATION

A t one time some unions were beneficial to society.
Unions improved the lives of powerless workers.
Unions were needed before the super highway system en-
abled mobility; before television and the Internet afforded
instant communication, access to information; and before
this country's fabulous community colleges made it possible for people to become experts in any field.

Today unions are a disease. Unions are antibusiness,
anticustomer, antiproductivity, anti-innovation, antiprof-
its. Unions make companies less competitive. In the same
industry, a well-managed unionized company loses to
the well-managed nonunionized company ... every time.
Unions strangle companies. Companies have gone out of
business because of strikes. Entire industries have disappeared or gone offshore due to union activities.

Everyone knows that unions are bad business. Company management knows; union management knows; pandering politicians know; of course, the union workers know. Union members know that it is stupid when a plumber can't unload a truck; when an electrician can't use a hammer; when a carpenter can't use a pipe wrench. Union members know that featherbedding, nonproductive work rules, and unnecessary overtime are scams they would never tolerate if they owned a business.

Most union members are decent people trying to raise their kids. Union members want to work hard, want to contribute, are proud of their company. It is the union organization, the union leadership, that discourages productivity, discourages company loyalty, and hates the hands that pay them.

Consider one union whose contract with its company includes lifetime job guarantees. Whether or not the company is profitable, whether or not the company can stay afloat, whether or not the worker performs, or learns new technology, or is totally redundant, or is a doddering old coot, the only condition needed to keep the job is to stay alive. Such a work provision is madness. The executives that agreed to such a stupid contract should be sued for management malpractice. Imbecility.

Unions don't know for whom they work. Unions don't know that it is customer money that pays wages and benefits. If going on strike restricts or stops the company from selling to customers, ultimately the company's survival and its payroll is at risk.

As a means of reminding every employee of the importance of its customers, and to improve customer service, and to be more customer sensitive, one Midwest manufacturing company stamped its paychecks with the phrase, "THIS IS CUSTOMER MONEY." The pay check slogan enraged the factory's union representative, who ordered workers to walk off the job. Strange mentality.

Here is how to fight unionization:

- Hire employees carefully. Get people motivated to work hard. Do thorough background checks.
- Treat employees fairly and with courtesy.
- Pay at market rates or above market.
- Constantly communicate to everyone. People want to know what is happening. They want to know the company's strategy, competitiveness, innovativeness.
- Ask employees for ideas on increasing sales, cutting unnecessary costs, reducing waste, improving quality. Acknowledge all ideas. Act upon the doable ideas. Give awards, recognition.
- Employees have families. Don't let the job interfere with family life.
- Obliterate visible lines between management and workers. Get rid of executive washrooms, executive

dining rooms, executive parking spaces, private entrances, ginormous offices.

- Provide continuous job training and new skills training.
- Deliberately and methodically cross-train employees to do different jobs in the company. Teach valet parkers to be waiters. Teach PhD R&D chemists to be sales people. Teach machinists to be truck drivers and vice versa. Cross-training enables a company to reduce or avoid layoffs when the economy tanks.
- Remove frustrations and policies that hamper the people from doing their best.
- Get good and able counsel to fight unionization.
- Educate people to the true perils of strikes and work stoppages. Give true historical examples of how disastrous strikes have resulted in lost jobs and lost wages never recovered, created thriving new competitors, and closed companies.
- Fire troublemakers.

The alternative to unions is a workforce of well-trained, well-compensated, fairly treated, empowered, praised, listened-to workers.

Good workers, contributors, thinkers don't need to be in unions. Getting and keeping great employees is the best antidote to unionization.

PEOPLE ARE NOT THE MOST IMPORTANT ASSET

Irrespective of ad claims and slogans on trucks, people are not an organization's most important asset. Having good people is a strategy for creating, acquiring, and building assets. "People" is a collective, a changing organism of individuals. Individuals quit, get fired, die, retire, work hard, loaf. People are crucially important to the start-up company, to small businesses, and especially important to the one-person enterprise. But people are not the company's most important asset.

- Profitable customers are a company's single most important asset.

- Brand names are often a company's most important *intellectual* asset. The New York Yankees name is the most valuable brand name in the entire sports world. Team management could change every player and the brand name's value would not be compromised.

Here are some of an organization's other most important assets:

- Customer lists
- Desirable products
- Profitable market share
- Cash
- Trade secrets and intellectual properties
- Patents and technology
- Data and information
- Strategic real estate

Good companies build these assets. Tough times sometimes require tough people decisions. The fact that people are *not* a company's most important asset makes tough decisions a bit easier.

CHAPTER 28

NURTURE THOSE
YOU HIRE AND
ACQUIRE

H ire carefully. Hire slowly. Hire the best people possible. Then accept the burden of that hiring. Hiring someone, or acquiring people, is a great responsibility. The hiring company has the responsibility of making it possible for the people to succeed. That responsibility is directly linked to a person's career, work happiness, financial situation, family welfare, physical and emotional wellness. This burden is heavier in the case of recruited employees.

Nurturing the best people contributes to enterprise success. To nurture is to provide clear goals, a safe and friendly workplace, good tools, first-rate training, and wise and instructive management. To nurture is to nourish, protect, challenge, mentor, coach, politely give constructive feedback.

Acquisitions present special people problems for the acquiring company. The new people come from different cultures, have different ways of doing things, are compensated differently. They will be suspicious, nervous, unsure of their fate. It is not easy to integrate acquired people. And it is oft forgot that the acquired company's value is a function of past and present employees. Good companies think hard about their potential new employees before the acquisition. Good companies are fair and treat the new employees as they do everyone else. They treat the new employees as they would treat themselves if the situation were reversed.

Nurtured employees are a fiercely competitive weapon.

CHAPTER 29

PRUNE ALL DEADWOOD

———

J ust as the gardener, to promote vigorous new growth and radiant blossoms, prunes the deadwood off the rose bush, so too do great leaders get rid of all deadwood employees. The deadwood stems on butterfly bushes do not produce flowers. Deadwood does not attract butterflies. Deadwood employees don't produce results. Don't attract customers. From the lowest-paid employee to the executive ranks, if he or she ain't cutting it, cut them.

Cut with care. (You don't want to lose a single potential hydrangea blossom.) Don't discriminate. Deadwood is deadwood. Cut with respect: that deadwood may have (note: *may* have) once produced the brightest of blossoms.

Pruning all deadwood makes it possible for the strong to flourish. Pruning sends a message: performance matters; keep growing; keep contributing.

Too much deadwood and the company, like the un-pruned rose bush, falters, and then falls.

CHAPTER 30

BULLDOZE ALL
SILOS

I n farming, a silo is an isolated tower used to store
grain or fodder (food for livestock).

In business parlance, a silo is a company division,
unit, or department that is deliberately managed to stay
apart from the rest of the organization. Silo executives
don't share information with colleagues working outside
their silo. Silo executives sabotage company-wide decisions if they fear that the decision or direction will erode
their independence. Like the Balkan countries, silos war
against each other instead of outthinking their competition.

Allowing one silo to exist usually breeds more.
Companies held hostage by silos are ponderous; vulner-
able to nimble, committed competitors; unable to deal
with change; weak in new product development. Silo

companies employ more people than they need; have layers and layers of unnecessary, overpaid executives; and have lower revenues per employee than the leaders in their industry. They are fatally inefficient.

For thirty years, General Motors had more silos than Nebraska. Insular management, plus silos, rotted General Motors from within. Buick stole sales from Cadillac. GMC trucks cannibalized Suburbans. Wholly-owned divisions that made car parts deliberately overcharged the divisions that assembled Olds, Corvette, and Chevrolet, making their own corporation noncompetitive. The branded car divisions all had different accounting departments, ad agencies, computer systems. All divisions fought efficiency and fought eliminating redundancies, even though it would save millions of dollars. Protecting the silo came before the good of the company.

Silos, like medieval fiefdoms, are managed by self-crowned royalty. Bulldozing the silos starts with changing the people who run the fiefdoms. If those kings and duchesses and lords don't immediately dismantle their silos and their attendant moat-like cultural mindsets, fire them.

Fire every single executive who does not really join the team.

Be unflinching. There are plenty of people in the organization who can be promoted and who will do a better job. You have nothing to lose—except more money, more customers, more market share.

74

CHAPTER 31

BROOM OUT ALL
BUREAUCRACY

T he word *bureaucracy* is of French origin. It means "an administrative system in which the need or inclination to follow rigid or complex procedures impedes effective action." Bureaucracy is antisimplicity and anti–common sense.

In governments, bureaucracy is obvious. Governments have cabinets, departments, agencies, commissions, offices, standing committees, czars, and endless alphabet acronyms—FCC, FDA, IRS, WFC—that deliberately delay, replicate, duplicate, obfuscate, perpetuate. Governments even have bureaus, as in the Bureau of Indian Affairs.

The bad news is that bureaucracy is less obvious and more insidious in companies than in governments, and more harmful. (Governments raise taxes to pay for their incompetence. Competition does not allow bloated companies to raise prices to cover waste and inefficiency.)

The good news is that companies can broom out bureaucracy. The trick is identifying the disease.

In companies and organizations, the symptoms of wasted bureaucracy include:

- Documents requiring more than two signatures.
- Assistants to the executive assistant.
- More than ten to twelve people reporting to the COO.
- A budget line item for "corporate presentations."
- A requirement that someone in addition to the sales manager (or any manager) approve sales force expense accounts.
- People who cannot say in ten seconds how their job gets and keeps customers, today or tomorrow.
- Functions that are not core or crucial to what the company does, or how it makes money. How can an in-house travel agency be more efficient than an independent agency that competes for business?
- Policies that fetter, confuse, intimidate, or frustrate good, honest, well-hired people in doing their jobs.
- Endless "stages and gates" to navigate to make something happen.
- A need to take more than one day to present anything to management.

- Lots of different kinds of monthly reports.
- High-ranked decision-making or decision-approving committees, of ten people or more, which meet once a month. Absolute death.

There is a university whose faculty has so many committees they actually have a Committees Committee. By the time this school updates its course curriculum, the course is out of date and the teachers are dead.

Bureaucracy is bureau-crazy.

Get rid of it.

CHAPTER 32

Scoop Up Newly Available Talent

Smart managers are always looking for—and watching—the best people working for their toughest competitors, working for their most demanding customers, for their best-managed suppliers. Economic downturns often put great players in play. Mergers and acquisitions blindly eject underestimated talent. Some companies cut personnel with an axe, not a scalpel, putting good people on the street. Top talent, frustrated by management, frustrated by lack of appreciation, are the first to leave, because they are the first to be hired. Hunker-down companies unbelievably release talented scientists and engineers (because the company is cutting R&D investments). Hunker-down companies cut sales commissions, advertising, marketing investments; this leads to talent loss.

Downturns are the time to strengthen your team, to add new DNA to your gene pool. Sometimes in a recession you can hire talent for less money than in boom times. New talent brings new energy into the company and raises the performance standards for all.

Be careful about hiring freezes; they can freeze out talent. Employee census freeze is good. Hiring freeze is not good.

In the depths of a 1970s recession, an excellent specialty products company was reeling. Revenues were down, orders were slowing to a thudding stop, there were no profits. Sales were $60 million and declining. The CEO and the directors brought in a proven team-building COO. In a few months, the new COO recruited and hired nineteen new executives from outside the industry—in finance, manufacturing, marketing, research and development, customer service, international operations—and jettisoned truckloads of deadwood. Four years later the company's sales were $199 million with profits of $26 million.

Counterintuitive, recession-driven smart hiring saved the company.

Be ever vigilant to spot talented people. Tough times make good people available. Hiring motivated, top-notch people is a winning strategy to weather tough times.

CHAPTER 33

FORGET ABOUT
PEDIGREES

Pedigrees, MBA degrees, third degrees (as in tough hiring interviews) don't predict performance. Resumes riddled with brand-name executives, brand-name corporations, and brand-name schools are not proof-certain the job candidate can perform, get it done. Never bias the hiring process by presuming that an MBA trumps the high school dropout. Never assume that a general is a better soldier than a corporal. Never think that "Mr. Everything" on campus will be "Mr. Anything" in the workplace.

Take a long time hiring. Give tests. Give trial work periods. Give temporary projects.

Get the right people regardless of where they've been, where they were born, who they know, for whom they worked, or what schools they did or did not attend.

Pedigrees are for dog shows and horse breeders, not for impact players.

CHAPTER 34

PAY FOR PERFORMANCE, NOT FOR ACTIVITIES

P ay for knockouts, not for punches. Pay for sales revenues generated, not for sales calls made. Pay for packages delivered on time, not for miles driven. Pay for new products commercialized, not for new product ideas. Pay for games won, not for points scored. Pay for good grades, not for hours studying. Pay for increased brand awareness, not for number of ads run. Pay for store sales, not for hours open.

It is logical that the more hours invested in studying, the better the school grades. It is logical that a high-scoring team will win more games. It is logical that the boxer who throws the most punches will win the fight. Logical, but not factual. To be factual, the immortal Willie Pep, the Will-o-the-Wisp, the greatest featherweight boxer to ever live, pulled off one of the most astonishing events in sports history: on July 25, 1945, he won a three-minute boxing round without throwing a single punch.

Performance is outcomes, not the activities that cause the outcomes. Hours open, sales calls made, miles flown, time invested, seminars given, products sampled, are not outcomes. They are business-getting activities, actions, tactics. If an activity is linked to improving the competitiveness and economics of the company, then it should be emphasized, enhanced, scrutinized, measured.

But don't pay for activity. Don't pay a house painter $50 an hour to paint a house. Pay for the painted house.

Clearly define performance, outcomes, the results of properly executed strategies. Performance is return on capital that is greater than the cost of the capital. Performance is profitable revenues, new accounts opened, new customer contracts signed. Performance is not the number of proposals mailed, the number of "requests for quotes" answered, or the number of patents granted.

Pay for outcomes, not activities.

Paying for performance forces management to define performance—for every single employee. Paying for true performance reveals the stars and the laggards. Paying for performance creates a culture of meritocracy. (Only the greatest singers, dancers, and actors make it on Broadway. If you can't perform, you do not get on stage.)

If someone is performing, praise and encouragement is the supervisor's role. If someone is not performing, then management examines the underperformer's activities. If an activity that always leads to performance — say, for example, pre–sales call planning — is not happening, then the supervisor insists that the underperformer start pre-call planning, and start doing so to the company's proven high standards.

Paying for performance begets high performers.

CHAPTER 35

Continuously Rip Out, Tear Out Bad Costs

S mart companies know the differences between costs, expenses, and investment. Smart management sees costs as money eaters. They see investments as money makers. They see expenses as nice to have but first to go in tough times. The definitions of cost, expense, and investment varies by company and industry. Generally speaking, costs are rent, taxes, energy, the phone bill. You can reduce the cost, but it is hard to completely eliminate it. An expense can be a newspaper subscription, free coffee, office plants, club dues. You can eliminate many expenses. An investment is compensation paid to product development engineers. Other investments are employee training, market research, advertising, travel to see customers, patent filings, trademark registration, talent recruitment, product samples, innovations.

There are hard costs and soft costs, and all devour money. A hard cost is warranty claim payments. A soft cost is an inefficient manufacturing layout that creates waste, scrap, and product quality problems that lead to warranty claims. Investments that reduce or eliminate both hard and soft costs are, for example, *kaizens* to improve production and machine operator training and to install higher-speed machinery.

Kaizen is the Japanese word for "continuous improvement." *Kaizen* was first introduced to Japanese manufacturing after World War II. It led to "lean manufacturing" and "the Toyoda Production System" (Toyoda Corporation makes the Toyota car brand). Every good company practices *kaizen*.

No false savings. No "lowest price" mentality. Cutting quality to "save" money—such as buying a lower-priced but less reliable fastener—always has negative cost implications. Lower quality makes products less competitive, leading to lost customers and lost revenue. Lower quality increases downstream costs, such as product replacement, more service and maintenance, lawsuits. The lowest price is rarely the lowest cost.

The connection between component or ingredient price and its ultimate cost is a slippery concept for many companies. It is totally wrong for purchasing and procurement people to be paid or given bonuses based on simply getting the lowest price offered in the market. Just as a world-class restaurant would never buy second-class vegetables, so too a paper mill should not buy a motor for $5,000 if the $6,000 motor runs twice as long.

Look for the clues that signal inefficiency, bad costs, waste:

- Units produced per manufacturing person are below industry averages.
- Customer complaints.
- Chronic late deliveries.
- Chronic partial fills on orders shipped.
- Obsolete supplier parts inventory.
- Scrap and throwaway.
- Sales people using selling time for email, paperwork, non-selling activities.
- Glacial decision making.
- Slow decision implementation.
- More factory square footage per unit produced than at competitors.
- Unions.
- Procurement people paid on getting lowest purchase price per item purchased.
- Warranty claims.
- Product recalls.
- Workforce paid below market.

- English not read or spoken by everyone. And for companies in Mexico, Spanish not spoken by everyone. Same in Russia, Korea, et al.
- Transaction costs that exceed $30. Companies have different definitions of "transaction," but typically a transaction is sending an invoice, cutting a check, processing a bill, reviewing a bill. Handling these transactions cost money. Companies that have transaction costs greater than $30 must investigate ways to bring down costs.
- Census of employees growing faster than sales revenue per employee.
- Sales per outlet growing at a slower rate than overall sales. (This might mean sales at new outlets are masking a deterioration.)

These are clues, not certainties. Nevertheless, tough competitors leap into fix-it mode as soon as any clue is discovered. No hand wringing. No "can't be's." No finger pointing. No endless committee meetings. They race to first patch the wound, put on a bandage, stop the bleeding, even if there is no blood. Then management works relentlessly to find root causes and to do whatever it takes to deploy a permanent solution.

Rip out costs. Purge waste and inefficiency in whatever form. Use the savings to develop and launch a new product.

CHAPTER 36

THE DO AND DON'T CUT LIST

Winning companies don't panic in tough economic times. They execute the management game plan they use in good times, at all times. Fearful companies frantically cut spending and investing everywhere, even in those areas that impact revenues, such as sales training and advertising. Mindless cutting of expenses weakens competitiveness and market position.

Winning companies *do* continuously cut:

- Bureaucracy in all forms, particularly excess layers of redundant management
- Waste, scrap, rejects
- Policies that constrain productivity
- Time to market
- Time to decide

- Noncore jobs, such as cafeteria, mailroom, and vehicle fleet management
- Meetings, email, administrative reports

Winning companies *do not* cut:

- Prices
- Customer-facing people
- Sales force
- Sales commissions
- Sales training
- Research and development
- New product launches
- Customer-tested communications, such as advertising

Good companies, due to great leaders, stay cool and calm in economic crises and have the discipline, conviction, and courage to do the opposite of what hunker-down managements do.

CHAPTER 37

Forget Monthly Reports

The ubiquitous monthly report is not sacrosanct; 97.4 percent of monthly reports are a waste of management time, a waste of paper, of paperclips, of ink cartridges. Monthly reports are ancient history. By the time they percolate up and through layers of management, it is already next month.

Depending on a company's political landscape, monthly reports may be less than candid. Any monthly report longer than one page is creative writing. They may be used to avoid or divert criticism or oversight. They may not expose mistakes that need correction. Few monthly reports lead with a headline, "I was so unprepared for the sales call on Big Customer that the guy told me to leave," or "Our competitor introduced a new product similar to the idea I nixed, and it is now beating us like a piñata bat."

Do the math. Let's say a company requires eighty monthly reports from managers, sales people, department heads. Each report takes at least six hours to research, craft, publish. That is 480 hours in report preparation. Each report goes to an average of ten people and takes two hours to read (if anyone bothers). That is 1,600 reading hours. Leaving out the time invested in writing response notes, the time to respond to the responses, and so on, and so on, this company's report addiction consumes 2,100 hours per month. That is 25,200 hours per year that this company invests in reading old news, instead of making news, making sales calls, innovating new products. That is twelve and one-half years of employee time!

Good executives don't need monthly reports. They are in the marketplace, in the stores, in the hallways, in the lunch room, on the phone. Good executives are asking, listening, observing, helping, participating, training. They walk around, talk to people, get the scuttlebutt. They know what happened last month and what is going to happen in this month. What leaders want to know is what will happen next month, next year, next decade.

- Cut out monthly reports, or cut them to one page.
- Replace monthly reports with short sales call reports giving sales cycle status and next steps.
- Replace reading and waste with selling and work.
- Make money, not monthlies.

Leaders want *next month* reports, not stale news.

CHAPTER 38

No Money, No Meeting

M eetings are one of the most pernicious thieves of selling and productivity in business. There are too many meetings and too many bad meetings. Good companies constantly rip out the root causes of inefficiency and waste in production, administration, distribution, and marketing. Good companies abhor waste, and because meetings are often huge time wasters, meetings are managed to make money and to overcome challenges. All work in an organization should be tied directly or indirectly to generating profitable revenues, to reducing bad costs, to avoiding preventable catastrophes. If a meeting is not about enhancing the company's economics, for today or tomorrow, then that meeting is a candidate for extinction.

Warning signs of a bad meeting:

- It's regularly scheduled, as in "the Monday morning staff meeting."
- A mob of people is invited.
- It includes disinterested or irrelevant people.
- It's boring.
- It's a rubber stamp.
- It's a forum in which nothing gets decided.

The right criterion for holding or attending a meeting is "How will this meeting make money for the company or the attendees or both?" How will the meeting spur marketing, inspire innovation, teach winning skills, sharpen messaging, improve quality, reduce costs, forge competitive advantages? It is the responsibility of the meeting owner to sell the attendees on why it is in their best interest not only to attend but to prepare and participate. The meeting owner must dollarize the value of the meeting, be clear as to desired outcomes, and ensure that the outcomes lead to economic benefit within a specific time period.

A "money meeting" is one in which you:

- Meet with customers
- Provide or get training
- Set pricing
- Solve real problems

- Make decisions
- Test quality
- Share important information and alerts
- Give assignments

In addition, money meetings:

- Take ten to fifty minutes
- Are irregularly scheduled
- Occur on Friday afternoons (as everyone wants to finish and go home)

Meetings must be measured in money minutes. Wasted minutes are lost money. A meeting that decides on the perfect motivational theme for the next sales campaign, or picks a memorable brand name, or optimizes pricing on a hot new product, is a money meeting.

CHAPTER 39

BE FANATICAL
ABOUT SELLING

One entrepreneur started his business by selling copy machines out of the backseat of a secondhand VW Bug. His product was an unknown foreign brand competing against an entrenched, iconic American company that had 80 percent market share. His motto was "Nine no's by noon, and one yes by nine." "Nine," he often said, "is my driving number. My daily gotta get." No office. No secretary. No cell phone. He had just one weapon, one advantage over the market leader: he could outhustle, outsell, outwork the market leader's top ten sales people put together.

Five years later his company had ten offices and 115 employees, 95 of which were sales people, well compensated almost entirely by commissions.

The founder was an instinctive marketer, a customer-getter, a sell-sell-sell zealot. He knew how inefficient it was to make cold calls on office managers and potential accounts, as he had to do when he started the company. He believed in advertising: running lots of well-crafted advertising messages designed to generate qualified leads for his cherished sales force. He hired a spunky little advertising agency, and he demanded that the firm's president accompany him to visit sales offices and customers. The advertising agency's president instantly noted something eerie about his client's sales offices: except for one or two very busy phone receptionists, the offices were entirely empty. Cubicles, chairs, desks, but no people.

"Offices seem kind of empty?"

"That's right. Between eight and five, I want my guys and gals in the field making sales calls."

"When do they make appointments, do their paperwork, that kind of thing?"

"They get good leads. Not as good and not as many as you promise to deliver, but enough. Between calls, and at lunch time, but instead of eating lunch, which is a total waste of time, they set up appointments. Before seven AM, after the day's calls, weekends, are good times for paperwork. We also use the offices for selling-skills training, some customer demos, admin. And I like having my brand name in big letters on the buildings. Customers see that."

"Okay," the agency man said.

"More than okay."

After visiting a number of empty offices the ad guy got the message: generate leads that keep the sales force in the market making lots of money for themselves and thus making the company more money. The founder made one last stop.

"This is our newest office," he said. "Couple of pros, lots of rookies."

Sitting at a desk, a salesman was talking on the phone. The founder stopped. He gestured to the salesman.

"Who are you talking to?" the founder asked in a normal voice.

"A prospect, a lead," the young sales person mouthed in an exaggerated whisper.

"Hang up the phone."

The salesman mouthed a silent "But—"

The founder charged to the desk, grabbed the phone, lifted it over his head, and slammed it on the desk top. He lifted the battered phone and smashed it on the floor. He kicked the remains into the corner.

"What's your name?"

"Brendan."

"Okay, Brendan. I never again want to see you in this office, wasting your precious selling time, your money-making time." He pointed to the window, and said, somewhat louder, "Your money is out there! Out where the customers are. You got it?"

The shocked salesman grabbed his bag and fled to his car.

"Where you going?" the founder called out.

"To see that guy on the phone."

As the young salesman left the building, the founder winked at the agency guy. "Sales management 101."

The incident quickly became company lore.

Twenty years later the founder sold his company for nine figures.

Remembering his "nine no's by noon" motto, "Nine is still my favorite number," he quipped at the closing.

Some companies forget that without selling, without customers, there is nothing. The fierce competitors are fanatical about selling, about meeting and listening to customers. In fierce competitors the employee census is concentrated in sales, marketing, customer service, and jobs associated with conceiving and commercializing innovation.

Every day fierce competitors are smashing phones and anything else that interferes with the way they sell.

CHAPTER 40

Don't Fire Sales People

First, a definition: a sales person is someone who generates more gross margin dollars than his or her total cost to the organization. The total cost of a sales person can include recruitment and hiring costs, base salary, commissions, nonbillable expenses, car, phone, insurances, retirement contributions, office expenses, sales management time and travel, any individual training. Sales people that more than cover their costs to the organization are profit-positive sales people.

Profit-positive sales people are desperately needed by every organization.

If, after a reasonable amount of learning curve time and good selling-skills training, the "sales person" does not cover his cost, then that person is not a sales person. He is something else.

A sales person who rings the cash register, covers her costs, brings in new business, and retains valuable customers is profit-positive, a rainmaker, a keeper. Incredibly, keepers are often fired, and too often for the wrong reasons.

Here are the reasons that justify firing a true profit-positive sales person:

- Cheats on expense accounts. That's theft.
- Steals anything from the company—postage stamps, supplies, information.
- Breaks important laws of God or man.
- Tarnishes the company's reputation and brand image.
- Hides important customer information from the company.
- Infects others in the company with his or her negative attitude.

The following reasons—although oft used—do not justify the firing of a profit positive, true sales person:

- Prima donna
- Doesn't perfectly know the products or technology
- Doesn't get along with colleagues
- Doesn't "fit in"
- Doesn't answer internal emails
- Skips important meetings

101

- Submits sloppy reports — or no reports
- Hard to manage
- Obnoxious, unlikable
- Complains, criticizes, whines
- Smells like a goat

That "the customers love her" is not justification for keeping someone who is not a keeper, someone who doesn't sell. That he can't read or write, but can sell like a ring in a bell, must suggest the question: "Where can we get a hundred more like him?"

Don't fire true sales people. Don't fire the people who bring in the money that pays for everything. Pay them, praise them, love them, hate them (but live with them), hire more of them, and train, train, train them.

And don't fire profit-positive distributors or resellers. It is dismaying that the major U.S. automakers closed profitable, well-run dealerships. Dealerships are a car makers' sales force. Dealerships invest millions of dollars in local market advertising. Closing dealerships means inconveniencing current customers, losing future customers, and converting thousands of once brand-loyal dealership workers and their families into outspoken enemies.

Firing thousands of proven sales people when you need sales is dumber than dumb.

Never fire that rarest of species, the honest rainmaker. Instead, find someone to find more such profit-positive true sales people.

CHAPTER 41

HIRE FIERCELY COMPETITIVE SALES PEOPLE

———

F iercely competitive sales people close new business in good times and bad times. Lots of ordinary sales people look good when the economy is good, because the rising river lifts all rafts. Good companies need great sales people in tough times. Tough times unveil the underperformers and the posers.

The one performance factor that distinguishes the rainmaker from the ordinary sales person is that he or she sells more. The rainmaker makes more sales and generates more revenue and does so in any economic environment, with internal operational problems or not, with higher prices, in sickness or in health. Rainmakers can come from any background, be of any age, any gender.

Contrary to the stereotype, rainmakers are often quiet, modest, understated. Don't hire them just on looks or a vivacious personality. Hire based on proven performance or high potential.

Here are some clues to help identify potential rainmakers—the selling world's rare killer competitive business getters. There are key identifying experiences and characteristics you can look for. Rainmakers:

- Keep score: they know precisely how much money they made last year, how much business they brought in, where they ranked among the sales force, what awards they won. Ask for those facts. Great sales people know the answers. Often ordinary sales people don't know, won't say, or will mumble bumble some answer.
- Have an inherent entrepreneurial streak and strong work ethic: as kids they were often paperboys, babysitters, lawn mowers, caddies.
- Can tell you about their first paid job (say, shoveling snow) and how much money they made on that job.
- Are motivated by money and peer respect.
- Are enthusiastic and fearless about selling to new customers.
- Sell outcomes, not products.
- Would rather make one preplanned call on a decision maker than a thousand cold calls.
- Most likely have played competitive sports.

- Read books on business and selling, constantly looking for new ideas.
- Love to be sales people. Are continuously learning. The best sales people, like the best athletes, absorb more in training sessions than their ordinary colleagues do. This is always true.
- Are never elitists. They know and appreciate people of all walks of life. They know lots of people and have different circles of friends.
- Are more optimistic than realistic.
- Are, for the most part, nice, courteous, funny, and fun to be around. Rainmakers believe their real competition is customer ignorance as to the values and help they can provide.

A fiercely competitive sales force is a hallmark of great companies.

CHAPTER 42

Banish All Selling Thieves

"Sales efficiency" is quantitatively defined as the amount of selling time spent face-to-face with customer decision makers, or phone-to-phone with decision makers if you are a teleseller. Effective sales people who spend more time in front of customers sell more. Anything that steals selling time is a theft of organization revenues and usually of sales person compensation. Any activity that steals selling time steals possible revenues.

A vending machine that is open seven days a week, twenty-four hours a day is 100-percent efficient. A vending machine that is open every day at O'Hare Airport will sell more than a vending machine at the corner of "Lost" and "Nowhere" in Smalltown, Planet Earth, but both are

100-percent efficient. Vending machine selling thieves are "Out of Order," "Truck Stop Closed," and "Correct Change Required."

"Selling time" consists of face-to-face selling, pre–sales call planning, and skills training. Activities that steal from selling time are big, small, obvious, invisible, insidious. The den of thieves includes:

- Weekends, holidays, sick days (It is okay, perfectly fine, and recommended that rainmakers spend holidays with friends and family, but if one person sells on a Saturday and the competitor does not, the Saturday seller wins.)
- Poor pre–sales call planning
- Poor prioritization
- Flabby goal setting
- Travel time
- Requests from management
- Chasing unqualified leads
- Customer cancellations and postponements
- Doing the job of others, such as market research and bill collection
- Email
- Nontraining meetings
- Lunch (without a customer)
- Bureaucracy, red tape, dumb policies

- Following up on late deliveries
- Paperwork not directly linked to getting and keeping customers (purchase orders are good paperwork; "activity reports" are bad paperwork)
- Intrusive, micromanaging managers

Some selling thieves are so ubiquitous and have been around so long, that, like Barabbas, they've become socially acceptable. After all, who dares criticize a sales person who writes twenty-page monthly reports, sends out tons of samples and literature, and predictably submits on-time expense accounts? But if a twenty-page monthly report takes eight hours to write, to print, mail, reread, correct, answer, then that monthly report stole one selling day.

Be on guard against the selling thieves. They are robbing you.

Here's a money-making, career-making rule: if while on the job what you are doing or are being asked to do does not directly or indirectly lead to profitable revenues, then don't do it. If you are working for an organization or a boss who does not understand, then you are working in the wrong organization, or have a bad boss.

CHAPTER 43

ALWAYS CONDUCT DAILY SALES MEETINGS

W hether the company has one employee or a million, everyone should conduct or attend a daily sales meeting. Whether the employee is a frontline counter person, a waitress, a finance manager, or the CEO, everyone must spend some dedicated time every single day thinking about growing sales. Everyone should proactively think how he or she, directly or indirectly, can do something to help the organization generate new revenues today or tomorrow. The daily sales meeting can be from one to fifteen money minutes.

A sales meeting is a money meeting.

Depending on the employee's job function, the daily sales meeting can include:

- Setting revenue goals for the day, the month
- Pre–sales call planning
- Reading a chapter in *How to Become a Rainmaker*
- Cross-sharing sales tips and techniques with colleagues
- Teaching how to handle an objection
- Calling company sales people and offering to help
- Practicing asking difficult questions
- Practicing how to answer difficult questions
- Brainstorming marketing hooks and promotions
- Sending a "Sales Tip from the CEO" email to every employee
- Acting on the CEO's sales tip

The daily sales meeting puts selling, meeting customers, prospecting, lead qualification, getting referrals at the top of everyone's mind. The daily sales meeting always leads to more sales calls, more deals closed, more revenue.

Investing ten minutes every day in a sales meeting will jump start revenues.

CHAPTER 44

THE BIG
OPPORTUNITY

———

G reat managers keep their best sales people in the field—selling, selling, selling.

Luke was on track to become his company's Sales person of the Year. He was motivated and working hard to win. The rules for this award were simple: he or she who generated the most sales revenue over an assigned quota would win. If Sales person #1 had a quota of $800,000 and sold $1,000,000, and Sales person #2 had a quota of $1,000,000 and sold $1,100,000, Sales person #1 would win. The quotas were fair and tough. The quotas were based on factors including market potential, historical territory sales, geographical size of the territory, and available selling days.

Luke did his paperwork on Saturdays. His colleagues did paperwork on Fridays. Luke made more sales

111

calls than his colleagues. Some of Luke's colleagues would occasionally wing it on a sales call, depending on selling skills and experience to close the deal. Not so with Luke. Luke meticulously planned every sales call. Luke outlined in writing what he wanted to achieve on each call: what he would show, what customer objections he might encounter, and what questions to ask. Luke's call-to-close ratio was lower than his colleagues.

One evening he received a phone call from his regional manager. "Luke," he said, "there is a big opportunity for you."

"Good. What is it?" Luke asked.

"It is a huge opportunity," the regional manager said.

"I'm game. What's the opportunity?"

"Mr. Big Boss, the company's senior vice president of sales and marketing, is flying into Omaha next Wednesday to visit customers. You can pick him up at the airport. Drive him around. Drive him back. That kind of thing. He's heard of you. This is a chance to impress the guy."

"Omaha? I'm in Kearney. I've already covered Omaha."

"Luke. I know you want to win Sales person of the Year. I want you to win as well. It will be a feather in my cap, too. But pick the guy up."

"I'll have to drive up Tuesday, then drive back Thursday. That will wreck three selling days."

"Luke. Listen. This is a great opportunity. Mr. Big Boss can help your career. You're ambitious. You should do it."

"If I go, will you reduce my quota by three selling days?" Luke asked.

"No. I can't change the rules for one person."

"Well, if you can't change the rules, I can't go. Send whoever is in second place in the sales contest."

Luke declined the big opportunity. He decided that being a chauffeur was Bad ROT—a bad return on time.

Three months later, about two hundred sales people and other managers gathered for the annual award dinner. Mr. Big Boss presented the awards.

When it came time for the biggest award, Mr. Big Boss began by saying: "Let me tell you a personal story. A few months ago I was out in the marketplace. I thought it would be a good idea if one of our bright young sales people could drive me around. I could get a better feel for the market. I was wrong. It is far better for a good sales person to be calling on our customers than chauffeuring me. Luke, you are this year's Sales person of the Year, and not just because you were more over quota than everyone else. You reminded everyone that getting and keeping and serving customers is our number one priority. You reminded us that our customers are why this company exists—that our customers paid for this meeting and fund everyone's paychecks."

Amidst applause, Luke returned to his table and sat down next to his regional manager. His RM shook Luke's hand. "Congratulations, Luke. You are a winner."

Luke's RM was an old pro. He had been a regional manager for decades.

"By the way, Luke, did I ever tell you that Mr. Big Boss used to work for me? He started in sales, like you." The old pro slapped the table and laughed.

CHAPTER 45

NEVER CANCEL
BATTING PRACTICE

Professional athletic teams, musicians, entertainers practice every day. Professionals work on the fundamentals of their game every single day. Every day they work to improve skills. If superstar athletes practice every day, so too should customer-facing people practice selling skills. There is nothing wrong with daily ten-minute sales meetings. There is nothing wrong with planned, thoughtful daily doses of sales training.

Everybody in the baseball team organization knew the boss wanted to cut costs. The boss really, really wanted to cut costs. To make his point, the boss cancelled all but one subscription to *Sports Galore* magazine. "Read it and pass it on," the boss grumbled.

Wanting to rocket-boost his career, a relatively inexperienced finance department manager pitched a cost-cutting idea to the boss.

```
To: Boss
Fr: Myopic Manager
Re: Dramatic Cost Cutting Idea
Boss: To cut costs, we should cancel
spring training and any other preseason
practice, including exhibition games.
The team would save over $5,000,000 in
expenses. (And boss, that's like 200,000
```
Sports Galore subscriptions.) The savings
would be in the following areas:

- No money spent on new bats, broken bats, lost balls.
- No travel to other ball parks.
- No per diem expenses to players and coaches.
- No hotel rooms.
- No payments to umpires.
- No maintenance money spent on fields and stadiums.
- No uniform cleaning.
- We won't need special skills coaches: big savings there.
- No brochures, printing of tickets, advertising.

- Huge savings on electricity with no
  ''under-the-lights'' games.
- And lots more.

Cost-cuttingly yours,
I. M. Adoppo.

You may think this cost-cutting recommendation is ridiculous, and you would be correct, but this kind of thinking happens every single day in even the best-managed companies. "Cut spending" crusaders constantly try to cut batting practice, also known as skills training. They constantly lobby to cut advertising, product promotions, sales commissions, travel to customers, market research, research and development, new product launches.

Such expense cutting is myopic. It makes the company blind and deaf to its customers. It makes customers blind and deaf to the company. Customers see and hear other sellers and decide to give them a try.

In addition to not cancelling preseason training, never cancel batting practice. Your people might strike out.

CHAPTER 46

DOUBLE THE TRAINING BUDGET

Perhaps nothing distinguishes the fierce competitors from the handwringers more than their overall approach to selling in tough times. Tough companies take advantage of those competitors that stop competing. The fierce competitors flood the market with sales people. And, like shrewd blackjack players showing two aces, they double-down their bets on sales training. Bold companies increase skills training to improve the efficiency and effectiveness of their sales people, sales managers, and customer service representatives, because proven training increases revenues. Timid companies cut training because that budget is cuttable, escapable. Timid companies cut because they can, not because they should.

Smart companies know that training returns the investment and generates significant return on that investment. Weak companies don't just cut training (and advertising and customer visits and support personnel), they eliminate training. Weak companies concede customers to their fierce competitors.

To cut training that teaches sales people how to get more appointments, handle the price objection, and close more deals is an inexcusable error. Smart competitors know that the biggest financial exposure, the biggest error, is to stop selling.

The training has to be effective. It has to make the people better performers. Good companies make certain the training works. For example, to judge sales training companies, look at these kinds of metrics pre- and post training:

- Average length of sales cycle
- Average selling price
- Average size of deal
- Number of sales per month per sales person
- Number of calls needed to close the deal
- Requests for price discounts
- Average gross margin
- Number of quality sales call per month, pre- and posttraining

Fierce competitors train, train, train so they can sell, sell, sell.

Big trainers are big winners.

CHAPTER 47

LOVE THAT CRANKY, FICKLE, DEMANDING CUSTOMER

The thousand year-old joke — "This would be a great business if it were not for the customers" — ain't funny. Customers may be indifferent and callous and temperamental. Customers can be cranky, picky, needy, impatient, intolerant. Think of those troublemaking customers who …

- Want great quality
- Want continuously improving quality
- Want lower prices
- Want products delivered at once
- Pay late
- Complain

- Sample alternative brands or suppliers
- Want something new
- Expect you to know their name
- Want you to stay open when you are tired
- Don't return your calls
- Require endless service

These overbearing customers are also those who ...

- Pay your prices
- Pay your salary
- Pay your rent
- Pay your insurance bills
- Tell a friend nice things about you
- Are unexpectedly fair when something goes wrong
- Give referrals
- Remember the gracious gesture
- Love happy surprises
- Return again and again

Cranky or cantankerous matters not. Cranky customers can crank the cash register. If the customer is profitable and does not negatively impact your company or employees, then that customer is your company's best friend.

Good companies love their best friends. Good companies tirelessly identify and woo all the friends they can.

CHAPTER 48

FIRE THE "STRATEGIC CUSTOMER"

Not all customers are good customers. A customer that costs more to acquire, more to support, to maintain, to service than the revenues generated is not a good customer. Good customers are those who are net profitable to the company.

Some companies use the euphemism "strategic" to rationalize why they are doing business with a customer who reduces profits rather than adds to profits. "Strategic customers" are often big, well-known companies. The selling company likes to brag that they are doing business with XYZ, Inc. Sometimes the significant revenues from XYZ, Inc. blind management to the true worth of the customer.

The strategic account may not be profitable if that customer:

- Makes constant demands for ever lower prices
- Doesn't appreciate your value proposition
- Treats your product as a commodity
- Forces sales people to call on the "commodity buyer"
- Gives your products or designs to your competitors
- Pays bills in sixty to ninety days, while taking the 2-percent discount offered for payment in ten days
- Expects their shipment needs and requirements to come first
- Gives zero to little credit for emergency shipments, expedited shipments
- Puts every product, every project out to bid
- Absorbs an inordinate amount of engineering time
- Requires special production machinery to make the products
- Uses more office space, or factory floor space, or warehouse space per unit sold than other customers
- Requires more people to manage the account on a per-unit basis than other customers
- Quibbles over billing
- Requires significant amounts of work-in-process and finished goods inventories

Such clues signal the need to do a fully allocated cost analysis. If, after deducting sales costs, sales commissions, cost of late payments, cost of inventory, and such, there is a net loss on the customer, then fire the customer.

Give your competitors a present. Let them have the strategic account. Let the strategic account drain their resources while you redeploy to profitable current and future customers.

Firing a strategic account is a good strategy. Just ask the hundreds of parts suppliers driven out of business by the auto manufacturers.

CHAPTER 49

CUSTOMER SERVICE IS A SURVIVAL STRATEGY

I n a competitive industry, true customer service is a survival strategy. Have bad customer service, and the other company gets your customers. True customer service wins the second sale, generates positive word-of-mouth advertising, reduces costs, and increases profits. Customer service is part of the sale, part of the total customer purchase and postpurchase experience. Customer service is part of the product and a big part of the company's value proposition.

Selling gasoline to motorists is a brutally competitive business. To consumers, and to many gas station owners, gasoline is seen as a commodity. One brand of gas is the same as the others. Thus consumers buy gas where they can get the cheapest price. As overall gasoline prices go up, the motivation to buy at the lowest price goes up even more. Given this reality, it is noteworthy how one privately owned gas station, on an interstate highway lined with big brand-name outlets, sells gas at five percent more per gallon. At, say, $3.00 a gallon, 5 percent is a 15-cent premium.

The station is well-lit, but not as ostentatiously lit as are the competitors. The outside of the building is not as modern in style or construction as are the competitors. Compared to its competitors, the high-priced gas station seems quaint, a bit yesteryear. When a customer does stop for gas, or to buy food, or to use the restrooms, the customer service magic begins.

Two attendants immediately appear by the vehicle. One attendant determines the driver's needs; the other pumps the gas. No "self-service" here. One attendant invites the driver and passengers into the station. The other cleans all windows, mirrors, lights. One attendant checks the air pressure in the tires and freely fills any needy tires with air. "Would you like me to check your oil and brake fluid?" is always asked.

The inside of the station is like a hotel lobby: flowers, shined floors, espresso service, courteous greeters. The bathrooms are like those in the most expensive luxury hotels. More fresh flowers, new hand towels, perfectly cleaned accommodations, great music. The food for sale is interesting, fresh, high-quality, priced above common roadside fare. Designated drivers get free coffee. Limousine and bus drivers get free coffee, free sandwiches, and access to a long-term waiting room. There is a staffed information booth, maps of the region, restaurant recommendations.

The station is hugely successful and profitable. According to the owner, "When they built the casinos up the road, I figured that unlike before, when the highway was used to get from here to there, lots of people would use the road on a regular basis. We can't compete on price. We can't compete on signage. But we can win with service. I took the plunge. Invested in ambience, good product, and good people. I wanted to get customers to stop twice. And they do. Especially the limo drivers. They use the highway every day. And they spread the word."

Good companies calculate the revenue value of a repeat customer, the reasonable lifetime value of a customer. They invest in customer service not for one transaction, but to get multiple subsequent sales. Calculate the lifetime value of your customers. How many customers are needed to break even on hiring one "extra" attendant?

Great customer service means anticipating and satisfying customer requirements and quirks. It means having a ready and willing furnace repairman show up at midnight on Christmas Eve. Problem resolution must be easy, fast, error-free, anxiety-free, and super fair.

Customers are fair as well, and reasonable and honest. Being good to your customers builds a new sales force, a new advertising media.

Great customer service keeps the limos coming back, and keeping customers is the key to survival in tough times.

CHAPTER 50

WORSHIP AT THE ALTAR OF QUALITY

Great companies listen intently to what their customers want and expect in terms of quality. Customers define quality, not the sellers. Customers determine the need-value-price parameters. Customers are the final judges of quality, not engineers or quality assurance people. If a customer wants a bearing that lasts for two hundred miles, providing a bearing that lasts a million miles is not providing better quality; it is providing an unwanted, overengineered, and thus an overpriced chunk of steel.

Is a silver spoon of higher quality than a plastic spoon? If the picnicking customer defines quality as a low-cost, disposable spoon perfect for eating ice cream, then a plastic spoon is preferred over a silver spoon.

Customers define quality broadly. The product must perform as claimed. The product's value must exceed its price. The product must be delivered as expected. Post-purchase problems should not burden the customer. Attractive payment terms, Sunday evening technical service, environmentally friendly packaging, unexpected store dollars for next purchase are all part of quality. Customers want pristine restrooms, smudge-free windows, freshly brewed coffee.

The year was 1942. America was at war. Small businesses were struggling. There was little money for extras, and there was definitely little money for luxuries such as going out for tea and dessert. Yet that is exactly what people were doing in Gallatin, Missouri. People were flocking to a small restaurant named Mrs. McDonald's Tea Room because she served the highest-quality cakes and scones and pastries in the land. Her business flourished while others floundered. Mrs. McDonald's Tea Room boomed in those tough times because Mrs. McDonald worshipped at the altar of quality. In exchange for their spare and rare dollars, her customers expected the crustiest pies and peachiest peach cobblers. That's what her customers got. That's why her customers returned.

Mrs. McDonald is long forgotten, but her quality philosophy is not. Every great restaurant company follows Mrs. McDonald's philosophy. When asked her secret to success, how she thrived when competitors died, Mrs. McDonald gave this advice:

Serve hot food hot, and cold food cold.
Use only the best ingredients, the best of everything.
Always have everything spotlessly clean.
Present every dish as attractively as you can.
Don't try to do things like other people. Do things your way.
And work on Sundays and holidays. That's when the money is made.

Mrs. McDonald was a warm, friendly lady, yet a fierce competitor. Her winning weapon was adherence to uncompromised product quality.

Winning companies worship at the altar of quality and always serve hot food hot and cold food cold.

Note: There is no linkage between "Mrs. McDonald's Tea Room" and the fabulous fast-food giant, McDonalds... except that the Golden Arch people, billions of times a year, 100 percent of the time, serve hot food hot and cold food cold.

CHAPTER 51

GET RID OF
"MR. OUGHT-TO-BE"

___

When the customer picked up his boat, he asked, "Is the transmission fixed?"

"Ought to be," the service manager answered.

Hmm, the customer thought.

One hour later, out on the water, the customer heard the dreaded *thunk, thunk.* Back to the marina went the boat.

Days later, the customer returned to get his once-again-repaired boat. "Is the transmission fixed?" the customer asked.

"Should be," shrugged the inspiring service manager.

Barely out of the harbor—*thunk, thunk, thunk.* Back to the marina.

The customer stared at the service manager. The service manager looked back, shrugged again, and held out his hands, palms up.

"Call the owner," the customer said.

The customer outlined what the owner probably knew but the service manager and the mechanics had disregarded. The customer pointed out that he'd bought the boat from the marina for $34,000; that he had bought and sold some smaller boats; that he wintered his boats at the marina for $1,000 a season and purchased fuel; and that there were two other good marinas nearby.

The owner nodded. "I'll put my best mechanic on the job immediately."

"What's his name?"

"His name?"

"Yeah, his name. I don't want 'Mr. Ought-to-Be' or 'Mr. Should-Be' working on my boat. I want 'Mr. Yes' working on my boat, okay?"

"Your mechanic will be 'Mr. Yes,'" the marina owner said.

As the customer left, he turned to see the marina owner speaking earnestly to the finally concerned service manager.

Customers hate "Mr. Ought-to-Be's."

Winning companies have no "Mr. Ought-to-Be's" or "Miss Should-Be's."

When it comes to customer requests, great managers are "Yes men."

CHAPTER 52

ALWAYS LEAVE
FLOWERS, FLOOR
MATS, AND
FOOTPRINTS

Good companies are not shy about letting their customers know they love them, that they care, that they did and do good work, that they showed up.

Always let your customer know that you showed up, did the work, are still on the job. Let your customer know that you love the job and that you love the customer. This is especially true if you provide a service when the customer is absent or if you provide a work product from long distance. A highly successful office cleaning company rarely loses a customer, despite the 8-percent price premium they charge versus competitors. Once a month, after every cleaning, client decision makers arrive to find a fresh flower in a bud vase adorning a corner of their desk. Every month carpets are vacuumed so as to leave a distinctive pattern, a memorable footprint.

The vehicle repair shop that fixes the brakes, then vacuums out the car and leaves a "Thank you" floor mat, wants the customer to remember the next time a repair is needed.

A ten-person office stationery printer of forms, business cards, and notepads does not dump its products in the customer's lobby and send a bill. The printer organizes its customers' supply rooms and shelves, putting everything in easy-to-find alphabetical order: envelopes before file folders and pencils before postcards. The company keeps a running inventory for its customers, ensuring they never run out, avoiding costly expedited delivery shipments, and helping customers save money by ordering only what they need.

Olivia's business is cleaning and servicing those elaborate aquariums found in restaurants, offices, and homes. She does more than clean out algae; she meets the aquarium owner and takes detailed notes on the customer's opinions, expectations, favorite fish.

Olivia's important client was showing his aquarium to a guest. He spotted a small note attached to the glass:

"Say hello to Andrew. He's the yellow-striped fellow hanging out by the sunken ship. Thanks. Swimmingly yours, Olivia."

Olivia kept a customer for life and gained a new customer.

There are endless ways to let your customers know you care. Leave weekend voice mails, bring homemade cookies, make charitable donations in their names, let them be the first to know your company's big news, before they read it in the paper.

Customers love the personal touch. They are flattered to be treated a bit more specially. Let them know you care and they will care about you. Every little personal note makes a memorable impression. Impersonal mass mailings make trash.

CHAPTER 53

DON'T CUT PRICES

—

Price cutting devalues brands. Cutting prices on industrial products, those items sold by one company to another, cuts profits. Cutting prices on industrial products does not increase customer demand. Customer demand for industrial products is derived demand. This means that a company that sells bicycle seats to a bicycle manufacturer is dependent on how many bikes are sold. If the bicycle manufacturer is not selling bikes, it is not buying bicycle seats regardless of price.

Customer demand for consumer products is direct demand. The bicycle manufacturer sells directly to people who buy bikes. If the bicycle marketer cuts price, it undercuts its value proposition, permanently devaluing the brand.

Rather than cutting price, the bicycle manufacturer could introduce a lower-priced, lower-value new product, or give a free bicycle horn with a purchase, or extend the warranty, or offer a free annual tune-up, or be more generous on trade-ins, or include a video of the ten best bike trip routes in the country, or any one of a million other things.

Cutting prices cuts profits. For an industrial products company, a 1-percent cut in price causes, on average, an 8-percent cut in profits. Conversely, a 1-percent increase in prices raises profits, on average, by 11 percent. Good companies not only constantly add value but also quantify the value and dollarize what the customer receives. This allows smart companies to maintain and raise prices over time.

Product pricing must reflect the value the customer gets from the product. Thus winning companies constantly add value to their products. Values include:

- Cash for clunkers … if business, not government, makes the offer
- Extended warranties
- Twenty-four-hour service
- Free roadside repair
- Frequent user points
- Year's worth of gasoline with purchase
- Priority check-in
- Preassembled components
- Just-in-time, always-on-time delivery
- Delightful wireless-Internet waiting rooms

- Pleasant, smiling workers
- Money-back guarantees
- Kids eat free
- A toy in the cereal box

Don't cut prices. Do add value. Articulate that added value in dollars and cents. Be sure that value is greater than the product price. When value exceeds price, the customer has no purchase regret.

CHAPTER 54

YOU ARE NEVER
ON VACATION

———

"Some of Us Are Not on Vacation" reads an obnoxious bumper sticker on a landscaper truck tooling around a town where the economy is dependent on tourism and on awful vacationers. The landscaper must figure the grass is greener in his town, and the pesky vacationers, slowing up traffic, clogging sidewalks, are like weeds in his garden. Those awful vacationers are the paradise interlopers who spend money in a restaurant that the restaurateur uses to pay his fresh fish wholesaler who then pays the fishing boat owner who hires a landscaper who has a bumper sticker that reads, "Welcome to Paradise. We Love Out-of-Towners!"

Customers make the economy. No customers, no economy. No economy, no business. No business, no jobs. No jobs, no money.

The landscaper who is irked that he has to work while others play needs an attitude adjustment, or else all the boat owners and all the fish sellers and all the bartenders and gas station owners and water slide operators will send him on a permanent vacation.

Good companies are never on vacation, and if they sell to vacationers, the red carpet is ever out.

CHAPTER 55

LOCK, LOAD,
AND LAUNCH

—

Lock in new product concepts. Load the new product pipeline. Launch new products and services.

Tough times are the best times to launch new products. Customers are looking for value, for alternatives, to save money, to make their business more competitive, to better their lives. In tough times customers are more willing to change than they are when life is easy.

In tough times short-sighted managements "save" money by not investing in new product introductions. They make empty arguments: "Too risky." "Can't be sure of an immediate payback." "Better wait until things get better." "Blah, blah, blah." Overly conservative management is self-excused as prudent management. Managements so short-sighted that they are blind to the future not only postpone or cancel new product introductions but also actually cut investment in research and development.

The fierce competitors launch new products, new packages, repositioned old products, line extensions, new sizes, new flavors. Innovators launch old products into new geographies. They launch new products customized to market niches and underserved segments.

New products give the sales force a reason to call on customers and prospects. New products are a reason customers will meet with sales people, why retailers will give shelf space, why publicists can talk to the media.

In tough times, new products have less competition fighting for share of customer mind, for end of aisle displays, for sales clerks' selling time.

Do the homework. Do the research. Think it through. Be careful. Execute every detail. Watch the money. But launch. Launch those innovations. Get to the market first.

Lock, load, and launch.

CHAPTER 56

SUE THE BLANKETY-BLANKS

I f an organization or person(s) steals intellectual property, data, trade secrets, product formulae, customer lists—anything—sue them. If anyone counterfeits your product, sells knockoffs, pirates your image or body of work, sue them. If anyone violates your patent, leeches on your research and development investments, sue them. Sue the company, sue the management personally, sue the directors on the board, sue the thief's bankers, sue the guard dog.

Counterfeiters, knockoffs, pirates, plagiarists, and forgers cost companies and individuals billions of dollars in lost sales every year. These thieves devalue brands, destabilize pricing, and compromise distributors, retailers, resellers.

It is okay to imitate innovations and innovators. It is not okay to duplicate innovations. It is okay to absorb best practices into an organization. It is not okay to hack into computers to discover secrets. It is okay to not spend a penny on R&D (dumb, but okay), but it is a criminal act to steal one penny of the other guy's R&D investment.

Protect and defend your patents, copyrights, brand names, inventions, trademarks, embryonic innovations, research and development projects.

The second you learn of a theft, a breach, a counterfeit, a counterattack, call your lawyers. Call all to arms.

A successful new product—indeed, any profitable innovation—is the result of customer research, brilliant ideation, winning product development, marketing planning, brand-name development, product launch marketing mix, launch investment, customer feedback, retooling, selling costs. Be it one dollar or one billion dollars, every cent and thought underpinning the innovation is your company's property, your assets. It must be protected.

Lawsuits are expensive, risky, and an enormous expenditure and diversion of management time. (So manage and pay your lawyers for results, not hours billed.) But theft is theft. Whether the thief is a punk with a handgun or a sophisticated company with resources, if they are caught with stolen goods, or caught selling counterfeits, forgeries, phony labels, diluted generics, they must be stopped.

Don't let the dishonest get a free ride on your brand-name equity or pickpocket your development budgets.

Sue the blankety-blanks back into the Stone Age.

CHAPTER 57

WELCOME
SERENDIPITY

I n the mid-1980s a hotel chain looking for a company to supply a unique luggage tag mistakenly called a specialty printing company a thousand miles away. The little company—fewer than ten employees—did not make luggage tags but figured they could. A serendipitous phone call plus an opportunistic, completely open-minded management inspired the first cohesive luggage tag, which launched what has become the world's leading supplier of high-value luggage, coat check, and valet tags.

The stories are legion in which narrow-minded managements ignored or rejected internally generated ideas, only to see employees leave and build successful enterprises, or to have a competitor take the chance and win. Companies should concentrate on what they know.

But they should not be so rigid, so myopic, as to outrightly spurn the serendipitous discovery.

The fierce competitors encourage employee exploration of business-expanding ideas. If the ideas are not good fits, but have promise, the fierce competitors sometimes financially back employees' start-ups.

Check your idea files. Check your archives. Review old experiments. Maybe the market is now ready for one of those forgotten "too soon" ideas. Maybe yesterday's serendipitous discovery is ready to rock.

CHAPTER 58

Go Green!

G*reen* is the world's word for being planet friendly. Green is also an emerging and smart business strategy. Green means reducing environmental insults; reducing and eliminating negative impacts to the world's bodies of water, above and below ground, and to its air supply and lands. Being green is becoming a competitive weapon—which means the fierce competitors are in the forefront.

Educated customers, regulated customers, and pro-environment customers are either voluntarily choosing green products or are being compelled to do so, even paying price premiums. More and more business-to-business customers are insisting that suppliers be green or get green if they wish to do business. Consumer marketers, such as Wal-Mart, are making green a requirement for products it will put on its retail shelves.

Products made with recyclable materials are preferred over those without. Products made with decomposable materials are preferred over those made with recyclable materials. Companies that put less waste into landfills have lower dunnage and disposal costs. Companies that use less energy have lower cost bases. Companies that reduce and eliminate noxious gas emissions avoid fines and penalties, increasing profits. Industries that do not show substantial progress toward becoming green run the risk of losing customers. Companies and government groups have announced they will book conventions and conferences only in green hotels.

Decomposable hotel key cards will outsell plastic key cards, even those made with recyclable plastics. Packaging made of corn byproduct paper will go into low-cost "refillable" landfills. Durable goods and capital investments (such as cold water dishwashers and cold water soaps) that can demonstrate a positive dollarized return over the life of the product will outsell products with lower purchase prices but higher lifetime total energy, water, and sewage costs.

Green also means money as in "greenbacks," an old reference to the American dollar bill. Go green. Get green. Your company will make more money.

CHAPTER 59

BE A MASTER
GARDENER

W hat if a garden were a company, and the flowers, fruits, herbs, and vegetables were the people who worked in the company? If a garden were a company, then management would:

- Be certain of the garden's purpose (why the company exists).
- Plan the garden (the business and marketing plan).
- Invest in the best seeds and plants. (Hire the best people.)
- Use the finest fertilizer. (Nurture the people.)
- Make the garden environmentally attractive (a productive workplace).
- Manage the garden with the earth in mind (a friendly, green company).

- Train the beans to grow on poles. (Train the people.)
- Rotate the crops from bed to bed each season. (Cross-train the people.)
- Be vigilant in monitoring progress. (You get what you inspect, not what you expect.)
- Prune deadwood. (Get rid of nonproductive employees.)
- Weed. (Weed out the unwanted.)
- Stake the tomatoes. (Support the people.)
- Thin the carrots. (Thin management layers and bureaucracy.)
- Build fences. (Defend against competitors and predators.)
- Encourage butterflies and bees. (Always welcome outside ideas and pollinators.)
- Kill parasites and destructive insects. (Get rid of agents provocateurs.)
- Let the random sunflower grow and bloom wherever. (Serendipity is welcome. Rigidity restricts.)
- Be aware that every plant is different. Some require lots of care and attention; others are wild. Some are glorious in the morning; others bloom at night. Some are colorful; others are thorny, prickly. Some blossom early, others bear harvest in the fall. They are tall, short, attractive, forbidding, slender, round,

give shade, need shade. The Master Gardener knows and appreciates the differences. (Be open minded, tolerant, understanding of groups and individuals.)

- Live with the weather. (Control what you can control. Roll with everything else.)
- Walk around the garden. (Walk around the company.)
- Stop and smell the basil.

CHAPTER 60

SUMMARY: CHARACTERISTICS OF THE FIERCE COMPETITOR COMPANIES

C ertain companies consistently lead, or dominate, their industries. They are feared by their competitors. This is why they lead:

1. Outworking, outselling, out-advertising, out-innovating, out-hustling their competitors twenty-four hours a day is in the fierce competitor's DNA.

2. Marketing—the identification, attraction, getting and keeping of profitable customers—in all forms, in detail, is the driving culture of the fierce competitor company.

3. Getting and keeping number one or two market share in their selected niches is the fierce competitors' most worthy marketing mission. They legally, ethically, politely but ruthlessly and relentlessly compete for market share. Making acquisitions that are additive to their core business is a growth strategy, intended to increase and defend market share.

4. The fierce competitors know precisely what business they are in, and use that for positioning their products and company. And they stay in those businesses.

5. Procedures, processes, and methods, no matter how sacrosanct or successful, are constantly under objective review. Every piece of the business is subject to rethinking, reevaluation, and rejustification. Fierce competitors constantly innovate.

6. Product and service quality is a best-practice requirement. Quality is defined by the customer's perception of it. There is no compromise on quality. Quality is a marketing issue, not a manufacturing issue.

7. The fierce competitor companies are always making things better, no matter how good they are. They do not settle for "good enough."

8. Leadership is expected to deal with the world the way it really is. Reality thinking is mandatory. Candor, honesty, questioning, homework, debate, and hardheaded clarity are the rule.

9. Change is understood to be a constant. The fierce competitor knows that external environments are influenced by all kinds of factors, including competition. Change and the necessity to adapt are considered windows of opportunity. Fierce competitors do not fret; they think and act.

10. There is no illusion about the competitive environment. Fierce competitors recognize that the competition is out to eat their lunch. They keep good competitive intelligence, particularly in areas of cost reduction and innovation. Because they are innovators, their basic competitive strategy is to preempt the competition and put them on the defensive. Because they want number one market share, they plan marketing strategy with care and execute that strategy perfectly.

11. Fierce competitor companies have a characteristic common to great sports coaches and teams: they recruit the best people, train them carefully, and put the best players on the field, on the ice, on the

pitch, on the track, on the court. They get good people in all levels and job functions.

12. Fierce competitors prosper because of good people. However, growing employee census is considered a cancer. Good people, but not a lot of people, is the guideline. This means not a lot of layers, especially between the CEO and the customer. Bureaucracy is the enemy.

13. If a person is not directly or indirectly responsible for getting and keeping customers, fierce competitor companies consider that job to be redundant. Support services not relevant to the core business, such as cafeteria service and mailroom management, are farmed out to companies whose only business, for example, is cafeteria services. It is better to buy services than to staff for them.

14. Outstanding customer service is mandatory.

15. Fierce competitor leaders deal with ambiguity, the future, the unknown.

16. Fierce competitors understand it is better to own a market than a mill. Manufacturing takes direction from the marketplace.

17. The cutting of bureaucracy and layers and irrelevant activities is part of the fierce competitor's culture. They eliminate parts, reduce meetings, speed analysis, cut memos, cut paperwork, cut email, cut steps, free up time to make things

simpler. To compete, the organization has to be quick, direct, and nimble.

18. Fierce competitors value strategy and execution, not endless planning and analysis. Their three most important words in strategy are *execution, execution, execution*.

19. Markets are looked at globally and with a macro view. Fierce competitors consider global changes and scenarios. They put themselves in the shoes of their competitors, customers, shareholders, and look at their company through those eyes.

20. In a fierce competitor company, everyone knows the company strategy, abides by the culture, and helps to adapt and implement change, no matter how wrenching. Everyone knows how their company gets and keeps customers.

ABOUT THE AUTHOR

Jeffrey J. Fox is an accomplished consultant, popular speaker, and the acclaimed author of a series of hard-hitting international business best-sellers, including *How to Become a Rainmaker* and *How to Become CEO*. Fox is the founder and president of Fox & Company, Inc., a marketing consulting firm that helps companies and organizations increase revenues and profits. Prior to founding Fox & Company, Inc., Jeffrey was vice president, marketing, and a corporate vice president of Loctite Corporation. He was also director of marketing for the wine division of The Pillsbury Co., and held various senior-level marketing jobs at international firms. Jeffrey is the winner of *Sales & Marketing Management* magazine's Outstanding Marketer Award, the American Marketing Association's Outstanding Marketer in Connecticut, and the National Industrial Distributors Award as the Nation's Best Industrial Marketer. He is the subject of a Harvard Business School case study that is rated one of the top 100 case studies, and is thought to be the most widely taught marketing case in the world.

Jeffrey graduated from Trinity College in Hartford, Connecticut, and earned his MBA from Harvard Business

School. He served as Trustee of Trinity College, and has won several alumni awards including Person of the Year. He served as a member of the Board of Directors of Saint Francis Hospital, one of the nation's top 100 hospitals. Jeffrey lives and has offices in Connecticut. His website is www.foxandcompany.com and his email address is jfox@foxandcompany.com.